RXpert SERIES
Student's Companion

Hospital and Clinical Pharmacy

Rxpert SERIES Student's Companion

Hospital and Clinical Pharmacy

Prof. S. Balasubramanian
M Pharm
Former Professor
C.L.Baid Metha College of Pharmacy, Chennai, and
Ex-Principal
College of Allied Medical Sciences, Madurai.

Pharma Med PRESS
An Imprint of BSP Books Pvt. Ltd.

PharmaMed Press
An imprint of BSP Books Pvt. Ltd
4-4-309/316, Giriraj Lane,
Sultan Bazar, Hyderabad - 500 095.

Hospital and Clinical Pharmacy
by Prof. S. Balasubramanian

Disclaimer: The authors and the publishers have taken due care to provide the authentic, reliable and up to date information related to the subject. However, neither the authors nor the publisher shall be responsible for any liability for any damage caused as a result of use of this book. The respective user must check the accuracy from other sources too.

Published by:

PharmaMed Press

An imprint of BSP Books Pvt. Ltd.
4-4-309/316, Giriraj Lane, Sultan Bazar, Hyderabad - 500 095.
Phone: 040-23445688; Fax: 91+40-23445611
e-mail: info@pharmamedpress.com
www.pharmamedpress.com/pharmamedpress.net

ISBN: 978-93-90211-91-3 (Hardback)

Dedicated to the memory of

My beloved father

Mr. A.Rm. Sankaran

Preface

This book 'Hospital and Clinical Pharmacy' is the fruit of 43 years of experience of the author as a practising pharmacist. It is written in accordance with the new syllabus for the D. Pharm course [E.R 2020] implemented by the Pharmacy Council of India. It is definitely an improvement over the previous syllabus, with a lot of new topics and chapters. Many aspects of Good Pharmacy Practice are detailed here so as to prepare pharmacists for the modern healthcare sector. Hope students will find it useful in their practice after the completion of their D.Pharm.

Heartfelt thanks to M/s Pharmamed Press, Hyderabad, for bringing out this book in such a nice manner. My gratitude and Acknowledgement to the authors and authorities of scores of Reference books and websites listed on the last page.

- Author

Contents

Chapter – 10

Clinical Pharmacy

Chapter – 11

Pharmaceutical Care

Chapter – 14

Drug Information Center

CHAPTER 1

HOSPITAL PHARMACY

Definition

Hospital Pharmacy is an organ of a hospital where drugs are manufactured and/or purchased, stored, and dispensed, and their uses are monitored and also, drug information, education and training are provided to inpatients, outpatients, as well as to healthcare professionals by a team of highly qualified pharmacists.

Scope, Origin and Development

Long ago, a pharmacy inside the hospital was called 'Hospital Pharmacy', just like a pharmacy in the community is called a community Pharmacy'. These pharmacies merely managed the job of 'Dispensing drugs' to the patients with a prescription.

But modern 'Hospital Pharmacy' is different. Its scope is broader and almost covers the entire range of services with respect to drugs. Thus starting from manufacture to Therapeutic Drug Monitoring (TDM) and beyond, a modern pharmacist is expected to perform all services in relation to drugs at the patient level. Earlier, there was no other responsibility for a pharmacist once dispensing was over. But now, a great deal of services awaiting him, even after dispensing-viz-the clinical pharmacy services, where he has to obtain the medication history of the patient, advise the doctors in selecting suitable drugs for the patient, monitor the therapy, intervene if necessary to correct the course of treatment and offer counselling to the patient either during treatment or at the time of discharge of the patient. Apart from that, he has to provide drug information to the patients, colleagues in the hospital, and the general public visiting the hospital. He has to organise and participate in research programmes and educational programmes and offer training to health care professionals.

Thus hospital pharmacy and its organisation, its scope and functions have widened enormously because of its transformation from product-oriented service to patient-oriented service.

National and International Scenario

At the outset, one must be clear that the above-mentioned services are yet to be established in India in all hospitals. They are being made available in big private corporate hospitals and a few government hospitals. It is rather unfortunate that such an excellent service is very slowly established by authorities. Nevertheless, these services must be introduced sooner or later in India as and when people realise their rights and requirements.

Hence pharmacy students should study this ideal hospital pharmacy setup and be familiarised with its requirements and services expected from them as and when it is established in India. He must strive to achieve this in his interest and that of the society he lives in.

On the other hand, these services are well-established and available in many developed countries. USA, Australia, UK and many European countries are forerunners in providing these services. They started those services some 50 to 60 years ago and continue them today. Other countries like gulf countries keen to establish a health care system similar to the western world also have complete hospital pharmacy services except for manufacturing drugs in hospitals.

Organisational Structure

The organisational set-up of a hospital pharmacy starts with a fully qualified and experienced Head of the Department. He must have the necessary education, specialisation, training and experience in most of the functions of a Hospital Pharmacy. Thus an M. Pharm graduate with a PhD and specialisation either in Pharmacology, Pharmacy Practice or Clinical Pharmacy is suitable for the job. Alternatively, a 'Pharm D' graduate with experience is also apt for the job, as these graduates have adequate exposure to hospital work and are given preference over others in western and developed countries.

Various section heads with experience in relevant fields of specialisation support the head of the department. For example, pharmacy postgraduates and graduates with experience and endorsement by the Drugs Control Administration are appointed to the Drugs Manufacturing sections of the Hospital Pharmacy. Similarly, Pharmacy Graduates with experience in the analysis and quality control of drugs and formulations are given charge of the quality control section. The medical stores of the hospital are given control to pharmacy graduates with experience in dispensing drugs. In both these sections D. Pharm holders are also appointed in adequate numbers to assist with the works.

The Central Sterile Service Department of the hospital, which supplies the required materials in sterile condition to various departments, is also given in charge of a pharmacy graduate assisted by D. Pharm holders.

Once dispensing is over, the highly skilled and professional service, namely clinical pharmacy services, has to start. These services are also referred to as 'Pharmaceutical Care', which is defined as the responsible provision of drug therapy for the purpose of achieving definite outcomes that improves the quality of life of the patient. The success of pharmaceutical care lies in determining or anticipating drug-related problems and taking measures to improve outcomes, resulting in a better quality of life for the patient. Hence this section of hospital pharmacy requires highly qualified pharmacists with experience in relevant work. M. Pharm graduates in pharmacology, clinical pharmacy or pharmacy practice specialisation or Pharm. D graduates are appointed in this section. Adequate numbers of assistants are provided to carry out the enormous work involved.

The remaining services of a hospital pharmacy, like Drug Information Services, Education and Training, are also suitably manned by appointing pharmacy persons with relevant qualifications and experience. Thus an organisation of a modern 'Hospital Pharmacy' consists of at least nine sections, as described below in the form of a flow chart.

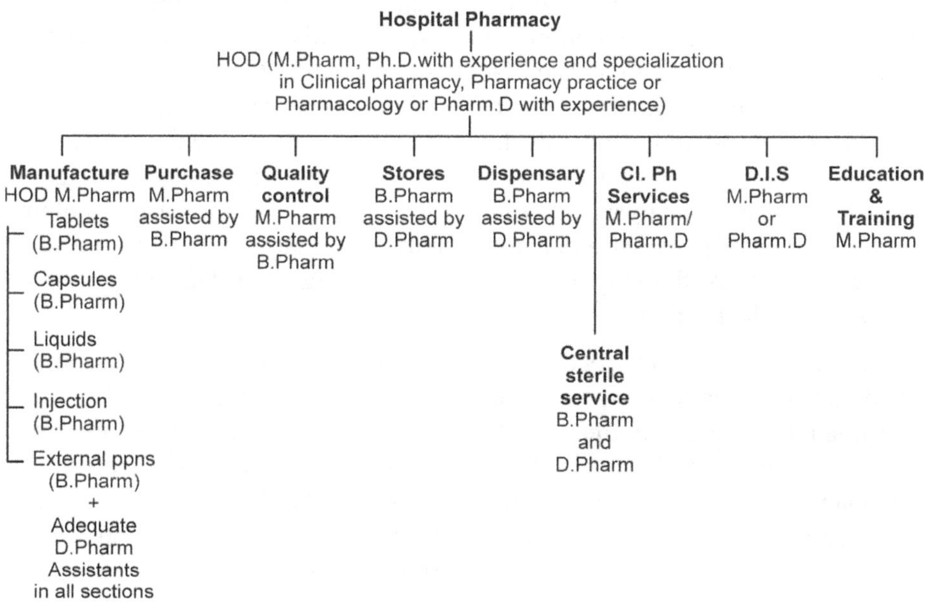

Figure 1.1 Flow Chart of a Modern Hospital Pharmacy Organization (With Technocrats and their Qualifications)

Professionals: Qualification and Experience

From the above organisational flow chart, we can easily list the number of staff required for a Modern Hospital Pharmacy. It is evident that this number depends on the workload or volume of activity of each section of the Hospital Pharmacy. Hence the first and foremost thing before deciding on the number of staff required is to fix the services which the Hospital Pharmacy is required or indented to provide.

In a fully pledged hospital pharmacy like the one charted above, there are nine sections, each requiring persons with some specialisation or experience in the relevant area. Thus starting with the director or HOD of the Hospital Pharmacy, experienced staff are required to head each section. The director or HOD of the hospital pharmacy must have overall knowledge of each section of his department. Hence an M. Pharm, PhD or Pharm.D with a minimum of ten years of experience in various activities of Hospital Pharmacy will be an ideal person. He is supported by a few associate or deputy directors with the same qualifications but less experience of 5 or 6 years.

The manufacturing section of the hospital pharmacy requires not only experienced persons but also the person who should have the approval or be eligible to get approval from the Drugs Control Department for the manufacture of the formulation concerned. Similarly, the quality control section, where the hospital-manufactured or procured drugs are tested for quality, must have experienced and approved analytical pharmacists. He should be able to independently handle and operate sophisticated modern analytical instruments and equipment. Pharmacists with experience in the manufacture and analysis of injectables, especially in Large Volume Parenterals [LVP], are essential for hospital pharmacy manufacturing units as these LVPs are the single most significant drug used daily in almost all the wards of the hospitals.

The next important section of a hospital pharmacy is the clinical pharmacy services section, where pharmacists who can provide advisory and consultancy services to treating physicians are essential. Hence Pharm.D graduates with experience must be appointed in this section. The clinical pharmacist also has to carry out the patient's medication history interview, therapeutic drug monitoring and patient counselling in this section. Hence few fresh Pharm.D or M. Pharm - pharmacy practice graduates should be trained in this important area of hospital pharmacy service.

Other sections like medical and surgical stores, purchase, dispensary, central sterile service and drug information centre should have regular staff with experience. The education and training section, on the other hand, requires well-experienced staff.

Thus all sections of the hospital pharmacy should be manned with suitable pharmacists, which is easier said than done. Hence the manpower requirement of the hospital pharmacy should be thoroughly studied and planned accordingly. Experienced people for each section are hard to get, hence suitable training programs should be developed simultaneously where fresh pharmacy graduates should be recruited as 'Resident pharmacists' similar to Resident Doctors or 'House Surgeons' in the medical field. These resident pharmacists should be appointed in all the sections of the hospital pharmacy in the rotation where senior hands are available to train, supervise and evaluate their work. Thus suitable manpower can be created in due course of time.

Infrastructure

In order to provide proper and effective service to the patients, good infrastructure must be provided for the hospital pharmacy. These infrastructure facilities can be as per the following requirements:

(a) All equipment and instruments for the manufacture and analysis of formulation as per schedule M of Drugs and Cosmetics acts and rules of govt of India. These are necessary to follow GMP and GLP as per WHO and USFDA standards.

(b) All the necessary equipment for compounding, repacking and dispensing in the main, satellite and ward pharmacies as per medical and pharmacy manuals and orders of Governments

(c) Proper storage facilities, including refrigerators and air conditioners with adequate cub board, storage space, floor space and lighting in the medical and surgical stores of the hospital. These stores and dispensaries should have separate cub boards with lock facilities for narcotics and other controlled substances.

(d) Central sterile service section should be equipped with the latest sterilisation facilities and storage area free from contamination with a laminar workbench, airlock ante room etc.

(e) As all above areas are continuous processing and /or storage areas and midway stopping of which may create huge problems, they

    (a) must be provided with uninterrupted power supply using generators, invertors etc.

    (b) A library with adequate latest books and online and database resources should be available both for use by pharmacists and doctors. There should be necessary facilities for data retrieval, storage, copying and recording. The new edition of Pharmacopoeias, a Textbook on Pharmacology, toxicology, therapeutics, biochemistry, microbiology, and drugs indexes, should be available in this library apart from professional periodicals (journals) on the above subjects.

(c) In order to maintain the above facilities, adequate clerical and non-clerical services should be provided. Hence a well-equipped office with stenographic bookkeeping people must be available. Needless to say, furniture and fixtures necessary for all the above activities must be in place.

Work Load

While calculating the workload for the entire hospital pharmacy organisation, each of its section's specific needs should be taken into account. For example, to calculate the number of pharmacists required to man the outpatient counter for dispensing prescriptions, the average number of outpatients per day has to be arrived at. The average time in minutes required to dispense pre-packaged medicines for a prescription has to be calculated, and then a number of counters to be opened and manned by pharmacists can be arrived at. It was estimated that usually, 4 minutes are required to dispense prepacked medicine and up to 14 minutes if compounding and packaging are required. If sufficient manpower is provided, the waiting time for the patient in front of the dispensary and the crowd can be minimised.

As per the medical/ pharmacy manual published by state governments in India, a pharmacist has to dispense to around 60 patients per day of 6 hours shift, allotting 6 minutes per patient. But in practice, due to various reasons like the huge crowd in government hospitals, disproportionate pharmacists appointed in our hospitals, a Govt. Hospital pharmacist is dispensing to 100 patients per day, and he is forced to work more than 10 hours a day. This makes the quality of services provided by a pharmacist to a patient to go down, resulting in friction, quarrel, dissatisfaction and disappointment to patients as well to the pharmacist.

Hence correct calculation of workload and its statistics assume importance to determine the manpower requirement. The workload has to be calculated for other sections of the hospital pharmacy, for example, in the case of clinical pharmacy services, at least one clinical pharmacist should be appointed for two wards and to provide round-the-clock service, 3 of them are needed. Similarly, to provide these services to outpatients, 2 or 3 clinical pharmacists are needed during OP hours. Other sections like central sterile services, drug information centres, stores and purchases require a minimum of one PG pharmacist and 2 or 3 graduate pharmacists as assistants.

If a manufacturing section is available in the hospital, it requires an elaborate production program and planning as in the Pharma industry. It may need the services of experts in material management and finance, which are dealt with below separately.

Pharmacists required for a 500-bed hospital with a full Hospital Pharmacy and 1200 outpatients per day:

Table 1.1 Work Load Statistics- Manpower Requirement

S. NO	SECTION/ DESIGNATION	NUMBER OF M.PHARM OR PHARM.D	NUMBER OF B.PHARM	NUMBER OF D.PHARM	TOTAL
1.	H.O.D/ DIRECTOR	1 [M.PHARM OR PHARM.D, AND PH. D]	-	-	1
2.	DEPUTY DIRECTOR [PRODUCTION, Q.C, CSS]	1[M.PHARM]	-	-	1
3.	DEPUTY DIRECTOR [CL.PH, DIC, EDUCATION]	1[PHARM. D]	-	-	1
4.	DEPUTY DIRECTOR [PURCHASE, STORES, DISPENSARY]	1[M.PHARM]	-	-	1
5.	MANUFACTURE	1[M.PHARM]	5	12	18
6.	QUALITY CONTROL	1[M.PHARM]	2	-	3
7.	CENTRAL STERILE SERVICE	--	1	2	3
8.	CLINICAL PHARMACY SERVICE	12[PHARM.D]	-	-	12
9.	DRUG INFORMATION CENTRE	1[PHARM. D]	3	-	4
10.	PURCHASE AND STORES	1[M.PHARM]	3	6	10
11.	DISPENSARY	-	3	20	23
	TOTAL	20	17	40	77

Job specifications

As described in the flowchart above, each section of the modern hospital pharmacy performs a specific function assigned to it. The following are some of the functions of each section.

1. Manufacturing Section
   (i) It estimates the annual demand for each drug used in the hospital.
   (ii) Plan the production schedule.

(iii) Manufacture the required items as per plan after purchasing needed raw materials, packing materials etc.

(iv) Carry out any special work entrusted to it, like, preparation of IV admixture, total parental nutrition etc.

(v) Check the standards of formulations by QC and QA departments.

2. Purchase Section

(i) Estimate the demand or the quantity of drugs required.

(ii) Specifications for the needed drugs are arrived at in consultation with the departments concerned. This includes quality, quantity, packing, strength, etc.

(iii) Follow the approved purchase procedure, like calling for tenders and quotations, and identifying the supplier to place orders.

(iv) Receive, verify and dispatch the drugs to the quarantine area and then to stores after approval by the quality control section.

(v) Settle the bills and be ready for any emergency purchases.

3. Quality Control Section

(i) It keeps ready the methods of analysis, equipment, chemicals and other requirements for almost all drugs either manufactured or purchased by the hospital.

(ii) Draw samples from the manufacturing section or quarantine area if purchased from outside.

(iii) Analyse and submit its report to the people concerned. Thus certifying the quality of drugs used in the hospital.

(iv) Undertake research and development studies with respect to the drugs manufactured in the hospital in order to improve their efficacy as well as to reduce the cost.

(v) Send samples to outside laboratories if they cannot be analysed by it.

4. Stores Section

(i) It receives drugs from either the manufacturing section or the purchasing department.

(ii) Store them properly until issued to the dispensary and other places, according to specified storage conditions, so as to preserve their efficacy and potency.

(iii) Issue drugs to dispensaries and other departments as per their approved indents.

(iv) Keep an account for all input and output as well as stock on hand (inventory control).

(v) Monitor the drug use pattern to inform and assist the authorities and manufacturing section in the production plan or purchase plan.

(vi) Look for the expiry date of all items stored, periodically and physically and bring to the notice of people concerned about near or short-expiry items so as to either use them earlier or return them to the supplier.

5. Dispensary

(i) Receive the drugs required for dispensing to outpatients in sufficient quantities from the stores of the hospital.

(ii) Be ready with pre-packing or repacking of drugs for dispensing.

(iii) Dispense them to patients by following high standards of dispensing like auxiliary labels, proper packing and instructions written on the envelope apart from clear and louder oral instructions.

(iv) Maintain account for the drugs issued on a daily basis.

(v) Provide a clean, neat and comfortable environment for the patients waiting to get their drugs.

6. Central Sterile Supply Department

(i) Procure, install and maintain all the required sterilisation equipment.

(ii) Prepare, update stock and maintain an inventory of items, equipment and instruments required by various departments of the hospital.

(iii) Sterilize the required items, as per the SOP prepared earlier and supply them to needed departments.

(iv) Prepare and circulate educative literatures to all the departments concerned on infection control as well as on maintenance of sterility and sterile area upkeeping.

(v) Always keep ready the emergency ward supplies.

7. Clinical Pharmacy Services

(i) Adequate numbers of clinical pharmacists are engaged wherever needed, including outpatient departments and all wards.

(ii) Conduct medication history interviews for all or specific patients admitted to the hospital and forwarded the relevant details to the treating physician or surgeon.

(iii) Identify the drugs brought to the hospital by the patients and give guidance either to use or discard them or forward them to the doctor.

(iv) After diagnosis, the clinical pharmacist is required to give his expert opinion on the suitable drug formulation and dose for the particular patient to the treating doctor if solicited.

(v) Once treatment commences, he has to monitor the patient for the effects of drugs by conducting necessary pharmacokinetic tests on his blood, body fluids and other samples. Based on these tests, he can recommend to the doctor to change the medicine, reduce or increase the dose or altogether stop the medicine. Adverse drug reactions are particularly monitored in patients who are on long time treatment.

(vi) He has to counsel the patients, as and when necessary, during the course of treatment or at the time of his discharge from the hospital. Provide the patient with the necessary medicines and instructions to continue the treatment or recovery at home.

(vii) Receive and maintain the feedback sent by patients after discharge.

8. Drug Information Services

(i) Pharmacist in charge of this service is required to collect, arrange and provide whatever drug information is needed by public or health care professionals or research students.

(ii) Update the information available to him periodically.

(iii) Prepare and circulate literature, brochures, bulletins or circulars on all important matters with respect to the drug's use to all the people concerned.

9. Education and Training Services

(i) Provide education and training to student pharmacists, student nurses, student doctors and even to other healthcare employees of the hospital.

(ii) Undertake educational programs for the public.

(iii) Accept and deliver lectures in professional associations and other clubs like Lions club, Rotary club etc., on drug-related matters and also on public health issues.

Interprofessional Relationship

Pharmacists are required to maintain a good relationships with other professionals working in the hospital, like doctors, nurses, lab technologists and even with administrative and sub-staff for the successful practice of their profession. Doctors and nurses are directly in contact with the pharmacy in their day-to-day activity, hence pharmacists should maintain a cordial relationship with them. Though other professionals are not connected with the pharmacy in their daily activities, a pharmacist may need their services at some other time. Similarly, administrative staff and sub-staff are helpful to the pharmacist in his functions like the purchase of drugs, its inventory control, billing, accounting and in related matters. Hence pharmacists should be polite, friendly and easily approachable by all professionals in the hospital. Inter-professional collaboration with a specific group of professionals is explained in the chapter No.10

Good Pharmacy Practice (GPP)

According to WHO, " GPP is the practice of pharmacy that responds to the needs of the people who use the services of a pharmacist to provide optimal, evidence-based care."

To support this practice, it is essential that there is an established national framework of quality standards and guidelines. The requirements of GPP, as indicated by WHO, are given below.

Requirements of Good Pharmacy Practice

GPP requires that a Pharmacist's first concern in all settings is the welfare of patients

GPP requires that the core of the pharmacy activity is to help patients make the best use of medicine. Fundamental functions include the supply of medication and other healthcare products of assured quality, the provision of appropriate information and advice to the patient, administration of medication when required, and the monitoring of the effects of medication use.

GPP requires that an integral part of the pharmacist's contribution is the promotion of rational and economical prescribing, as well as dispensing

GPP requires that the objective of each element of pharmacy service is relevant to the patient, is clearly defined and is effectively communicated to all those involved. Multidisciplinary collaboration among healthcare professionals is the key factor for successfully improving patient safety.

Good Pharmacy Practice guidelines were published by WHO long ago. It is mainly suitable for developed countries. Hence other countries were set to liberty to frame their own GPP depending on the local conditions. Thus many countries, including our neighbours, Srilanka and Malaysia, have their own GPP guidelines. In India, Indian Pharmaceutical Association [IPA] published GPP guidelines as early as 2002. From that, the salient points or topics are given below with due acknowledgement:

The guidelines are classified into two sections. 1. Structure guidelines and 2. Process guidelines

1. Structure Guidelines

   These refer to the pharmacy as an organisation and give standards/guidelines for

   1. Facilities
   2. Premises
   3. Furniture and fixtures
   4. Equipment
   5. Personnel
   6. Systems
   7. Quality policy
   8. Service policy
   9. Staff training policy
   10. Complaints policy
   11. Drug Recall policy
   12. Audit policy
   13. Documentation system

   Structure guidelines aim to create suitable conditions for the process guidelines.

2. Process guidelines

   These refer to the provision of pharmaceutical care and lay down the guidelines for:

   1. Procurement &inventory management
   2. Storage inventory management
   3. Prescription handling
   4. Dispensing
   5. Information for the patient
   6. Patient counselling
   7. Health promotion & ill health prevention
   8. Pharmacovigilance
   9. Enhancement of the professional role
   10. Professional interaction

   Out of the above 23 guidelines few guidelines are very important for the majority of fresh, new entrant, and junior pharmacists for starting their practice of the profession; hence they are reproduced below to be familiar with from the beginning of their career. Other guidelines can be referred to and learned by the pharmacists when required or in due course.

1. **Storage management**

   All products coming into the pharmacy should initially be quarantined, preferably in a separate area, before they are checked for correctness of quality, batch number, expiry, integrity, etc. After necessary checks, they should be transferred to their respective storage location. All drugs should be stored at stipulated temperature areas and protected from excessive light, dust, and humidity. The temperature at various areas should be recorded at predetermined periodicity, and daily records should be preserved for a period of 2 years. They may be correlated with the subsequent years' corresponding data to improve arrangements for the maintenance of temperatures.

   The medicines and shelves should be maintained clean and dust free at all times by following cleaning schedules and SOPs. Prescription drugs should be kept in such a manner that they are out of reach of clients. All the drugs that are to be stored at a 'cold' temperature should be kept in the refrigerator unless the ambient temperature in the area is cold enough. Drug and dosage forms that require special care while dispensing (e.g. drugs specified under schedule X, Narcotic Drugs and Psychotropic Substances Act and some other CNS drugs etc.) should be kept under lock and key. The key for this should be available only to the Pharmacist in charge at the time. Records of purchase and sales of such medicines should be kept per legal requirements. Shelves should be checked at a predetermined periodicity to ensure the removal of drugs whose expiry date is approaching. An in-house threshold period should be set and followed from such retrieval of drugs from the shelves. The near-expiry products should be stored separately and disposed of either by returning to the respective vendors or by expanding their dispensing. Drugs, which have already expired, should be stored separately on a locked shelf bearing the label "Expired Goods Not for Sale". Care should be taken that such goods do not reach the client in any case. Expired drugs should be returned to the supplier or destroyed as per in-house procedure at the earliest.

2. **Prescription handling**

   The client must be made to feel attended to and comfortable by friendly gestures and ambience as soon as they come into the pharmacy. Communication should be opened in such a way that it encourages the client to convey his/her needs by producing a prescription or by asking for other products or advice.

Upon receiving the prescription, the Pharmacist should confirm (i) the Identity of the client and (ii) Whether the prescription is presented by the client himself or by someone on the client's behalf. The client may be politely requested to wait while the pharmacist reviews the prescription for (i) therapeutic aspects (Pharmaceutical / pharmacological), (ii) Appropriate for an individual, (iii) Social, legal & economic aspects, and (iv) Legality & completeness of prescription.

Prescription should be complete with regard to (i) Name of the Doctor, his/ her address and registration number. (ii) Name, address, age, and sex of the patient (iii)Name(s) of the medicine(s), potency, dosage, and the total amount of the medicines to be supplied. (iv)Instruction to the patient (v) Refill information, if any (vi)Prescribed doctors' usual signature. Any confusion, shortcoming or anomalies should be brought to the notice of the prescribing doctors.

Correctness of prescribed medicines

The prescription should be checked for: (i) Dosage: Whether the dosage prescribed is within the standard minimum and maximum dose range. (ii) Double medication (same drug or different drug with the same pharmacotherapeutic effect) concurrently prescribed by the same Doctor or by two or more doctors to the same patients undergoing concurrent treatment by more than one doctor. (iii) Interaction between the currently prescribed medicines, OTC medicines being taken by the patient & the medicines being taken from any past prescription (records of which may be available in the Patient's Medication Records). Any drug interaction likely to render the therapy ineffective or cause undesirable effects to the patients should be brought to the notice of the prescribing doctor. (iv) Contraindication: age, sex, disease(s), conditions or other characteristics of a patient that may cause certain prescribed medicines to be contraindicated. (v) History of overuse, underuse, or misuse of medicines by the patient. Any of the above as well as handwriting legibility problems, should be brought to the notice of the prescribing Doctors. Any necessary change made by the doctor should be recorded on the prescription, with the words "Changes made over the telephone in consultation with the Dr. (name) at (time) on (date)" and should be signed and stamped by the pharmacist. This exercise necessitates a trust-based professional relationship with the prescribing doctor. In case of any doubt, the prescription should be got suitably amended by the doctor.

3. **Dispensing**

   Filling the prescription

   The medicine should be removed from the storage area, counted and invoiced. In all cases, the final review of the prescription and the correctness of dispensed medicines must be personally made by the pharmacist. As a final step, the pharmacist should personally dispense the medicines, at which stage appropriate counselling should be given to the patient. The medicines should be packed neatly so that their integrity is maintained any medicines requiring special storage conditions, e.g., a cold place (2-8°C), must be packed in cold packs so that they remain at the stipulated temperature till they are taken from a larger bulk pack then they should be packed in a clean, food-grade glass or plastic bottle or a clean envelope and neatly labelled as provided under the lock. Appropriate counselling/guidelines must be given for the patient as recommended below under patient information. Conscious efforts should be made to ensure that the patients' waiting time is kept at a minimum while all the necessary steps are carried out systematically. This can be archived by several management options, e.g. by deploying an appropriate staff-to-client ratio.

Hospital Pharmacy Standards

Hospital Pharmacy Standards were framed by the International Pharmaceutical Federation (FIP) and adopted by the American Society of Health-System Pharmacists (ASHP). The standards devised first in 2008 were revised in the year 2014 and published with the title " Revised FIP Basel statements on the future of Hospital Pharmacy" It declares that the goal of hospital pharmacists should be to optimise patient outcomes through collaborative, inter-professional, responsible use of medicines and medical devices. It is a long document, the salient features of which are given below:

1. Hospital pharmacists should engage health authorities and hospital administrators to ensure appropriate resources for, and design, the hospital medicines-use process.
2. Health authorities should ensure that each hospital is serviced by a pharmacy supervised by pharmacists who have completed advanced training in hospital pharmacy.

3. All prescriptions should be reviewed, interpreted, and validated by a hospital pharmacist prior to the medicine being dispensed and administered.
4. Hospital pharmacists should monitor patients taking medicines to assure patient safety, appropriate medicine use, and optimal outcomes for inpatients and outpatients. When resource limitations do not permit pharmacist monitoring of all patients taking medicines, patient selection criteria should be established to guide pharmacist monitoring.
5. Hospital pharmacists should be allowed to access and document the full patient record.
6. Hospital pharmacists should ensure that patients or caregivers are educated and provided written information on the appropriate use of medicines.
7. Hospital pharmacists should provide orientation, drug information and education to nurses, physicians, and other hospital staff regarding best practices for medicines use (a best practice is a method or technique that has consistently shown results superior to those achieved with other means, and that is used as a benchmark).
8. Each pharmacy should have contingency plans for medicine shortages and emergencies.
9. The "seven rights" (right patient, medicine, dose, route, information, documentation and time) should be fulfilled in all medicine-related activities in the hospital.

The document is classified under six themes. They are 1. Procurement 2. Influences on prescribing 3. Preparation and delivery 4. Administration 5. Monitoring of medicines use, and 6. Human resources, training and development. Each of the theme's headings is self-explanatory under which relevant matters are discussed.

ASHP Guidelines: Minimum Standards for Pharmacies in Hospitals

This document explains the purpose and elements of care. It lists the elements of pharmacy services that are critical to safe, effective and cost-conscious medication use in a hospital as follows.

1. Practice management 2. Medication use policy development 3. Optimising medication therapy 4. Drug product development and inventory management 5. Preparing, packaging and labelling medications 6. Medication delivery 7. Monitoring medication use 8. Evaluating the effectiveness of the medication use system, and 9. Research

Standard 1. Practice management

Effective leadership and practice management skills are necessary for the delivery of pharmacy services in a manner consistent with the hospital's and patients' needs. Hence this section explains about pharmacy and pharmacist's services, including 24-hour pharmacy services, After-hours pharmacy access, laws and regulations, policies and procedures and human resources. Under the human resources, it recommends a professionally competent, legally qualified pharmacist with an advanced management degree like MBA. Finally, it lists the facilities required for the above services.

Standard 2. Medication use policy development

Under this heading the document deals with policy development, formulary management and drug information. How to disseminate drug information is also explained under the last heading.

Standard 3. Optimizing medication Therapy

To achieve this standard, the document elaborates on creating relationships with the patient, acquiring essential patient data and consulting with other health professionals about medication therapy.

Standard 4. Drug product procurement and inventory management

This standard can be achieved by following the guidelines described under this heading. They are, selecting sources of pharmaceutical products, managing inventory items and returning recalled, expired and other unusable items.

Standard 5. Preparing. Packaging and labelling medications

This standard is explained under the subheadings, preparing medications and packaging medications. The first one deals with compounding, sterile preparations and hazardous drug products, and the second topic is about unit dose packaging and bar-coding of unit dose packaging and point of-care administration

Standard 6. Medication dispensing and delivery

Under this heading, medication dispensing, delivery and administration are explained. Starting with prescribing, medication purpose [diagnostic or therapeutic], medication order and its review are dealt with in the first part, and drug delivery systems, administration devices, and automated devices are explained in the second part—medication administration by whom, when, how and its record entry are briefly mentioned at the end.

Standard 7. Monitoring medication use

By reviewing patients' responses to medication therapy and also by educating and counselling patients and families, this standard can be achieved. The first part review is well-guided with ten points which a pharmacist should follow to effectively fulfil his duty of monitoring medication use.

Standard 8. Evaluating the effectiveness of the medication use system

Assessing pharmacy services and practices by documentation of pharmacist-provided patient care services and medication therapy outcomes, workload and financial performance and improving the medication use process are mentioned in this standard. Medication use evaluation, medication safety, antimicrobial stewardship, infection prevention, and control are also coming under this standard.

Standard 9. Research

It advocates the pharmacist to initiate, participate in, and support clinical and practice-related research in hospitals. For that, it explains the policies and procedures, procurement, distribution and control of investigational drugs etc.

Thus the minimum standards for a hospital pharmacy are well drafted by both FIP and ASHP.

Introduction to NQAS Guidelines

National quality assurance [NQAS] standards for public health facilities are published under National Health Mission by the Ministry of Health and Family Welfare, Government of India. It describes the standards expected from various healthcare facilities. It was first published in 2016 and revised subsequently in 2020. These standards have been developed keeping in the specific requirements for public health facilities as well as global best practices. Standards are primarily meant for providers to assess their own quality for improvement through pre-defined standards and to bring up their facilities for certification.

The introduction to these standards is reproduced below from the above document with due acknowledgement.

1. Comprehensiveness – The proposed system is all-inclusive and captures all aspects of quality of care within the eight areas of concern. The departmental check-lists transposed within Quality Standards, and commensurate measurable elements provide an exhaustive matrix to capture all aspects of quality of care at Public Health Facilities.
2. Contextual – The proposed system has been developed primarily to meet the requirements of Public Health Facilities; since Public Hospitals have their processes, responsibilities and peculiarities, which are very different from the 'for-profit' sector. For instance,

there are standards for providing free drugs, ensuring the availability of clean linen, etc., which may not be relevant for other hospitals.

3. Contemporary – Contemporary Quality standards such as NABH, ISO and JCI, and Quality improvement tools such as Six Sigma, Lean and CQI have been consulted, and their relevant practices have been incorporated.
4. User Friendly – The Public Health System requires a credible Quality system. It has been the endeavour of the team to avoid complex language and jargon. So that the system remains user-friendly to enable easy understanding and implementation by the service providers. Checklists have been designed to be user-friendly, with guidance for each checkpoint. The scoring system has been made simple with uniform scoring rules and weightage. Additionally, a formula-fitted excel sheet tool has been provided for convenience and to avoid calculation errors.
5. Evidence-based – The Standards have been developed after consulting vast knowledge resources available on the quality. All respective operational and technical guidelines related to RMNCH+A and the National Health Programmes have been factored in.
6. Objectivity – Ensuring objectivity in the measurement of Quality has always been challenging. Therefore, in the proposed quality system, each Standard is accompanied by measurable elements & Checkpoints to measure compliance with the standards. Checklists have been developed for various departments, which also capture inter-departmental variability for the standards. At the end of the assessment, there would be numeric scores, bringing out the quality of care in a snap-shot, which can be used for monitoring, as well as for inter-hospital/inter-state(s) comparison.
7. Flexibility – The proposed system has been designed in such a way that states and Health Facilities can adapt the system according to their priorities and requirements. State or facilities may pick some of the departments or groups of services in the initial phase for Quality improvement. As the baseline differs from state to state, checkpoints may either be made essential or desirable, as per the availability of resources.

   Desirable checkpoints will be counted in arriving at the score, but this may not withhold its certification if compliance is still not there. In this way, the proposed system provides flexibility, as well as a 'road map'.
8. Balanced – All three components of Quality – Structure, process & outcome, have been given due weightage.

9. Transparency – All efforts have been made to ensure that the measurement system remains transparent so that assesse and assessors have a similar interpretation of each checkpoint.
10. Enabler – Though standards and checklists are primarily meant for the assessment, they can also be used as a 'road map' for improvement.

The following are the area of concern in a health facility. 1. Service Provision 2. Patient rights 3. Inputs 4. Support services 5. Clinical services 6. Infection control 7. Quality management, and 8. Outcome

Currently, National quality assurance [NQAS] standards for the following facilities are available: 1. District Hospitals 2. Community Health Centre 3. Primary Health Centre 4. Urban Primary Health Centre 5. Health and Wellness Centre [sub centre]

They are simply a long list of equipment and other facilities required for various sections of the particular hospital or centre. For full detail, students are advised to refer to the above document [1596 NQAS for PHF 2020 – 16 Dec 2021 pdf]

NABH Accreditation and Role of Pharmacists

National Accreditation Board for Hospitals and Health Care Providers [NABH] is a constituent board of the Quality Council of India. It encompasses relevant and comprehensive standards for allopathic hospitals, clinics and other health care providers. It has a separate list of standards for hospitals, small clinics and others. For example, it stipulates the standards under the following headings for small allopathic clinics which are having only OPD. [outpatient department] facilities.

The eight chapters of allopathic clinic standards are

1. Access, Assessment and Information [AAI]
2. Care of Patient [COP]
3. Patient Rights and Education [PRE]
4. Infection Control [IC]
5. Continuous Quality Improvement [CQI]
6. Responsibilities of Management [ROM]
7. Facility Management and Safety [FMS] and
8. Community Participation and Integration [CPI]

Benefits of Accreditation

(a) Patients are the biggest beneficiary as the implementation of accreditation standards ensure patient safety, commitment to quality care outcomes

(b) Improves patient specification and increases community confidence as services are provided by credentialed medical staff

(c) Accreditation status provides a good marketing advantage in the competitive healthcare

(d) Accreditation provides an objective system of empanelment by insurance and other third parties.

Role of Pharmacists in NABH Accreditation

Whenever a Hospital or Clinic applies for NABH accreditation, it should comply and be ready with the standards prescribed for each section of a hospital. The pharmacy of the hospital is no exemption; it should also prepare itself for the inspection by the NABH team. All the pharmacists starting from the chief pharmacist of the hospital has a definite role to fulfil and succeed in obtaining NABH accreditation for the hospital. The following are the standards that are applicable to the pharmacy.

Policies and Procedures: There should be a documented policy and procedures for a pharmacy to function properly, and those policies should comply with the acts, rules and regulations of the government. The following are a few of those acts:

A] Pharmacy act B] Drugs and Cosmetics act C] Narcotics and Psychotropic substances act D] Drugs and Magic remedies act [Objectionable advertisements act]

There should be a Registered Pharmacist for dispensing and managing the pharmacy and whose Registration certificate should be prominently displayed in the pharmacy. Policies for almost all activities of the pharmacy is given in the NABH document, and they are about 1. Procurement 2. Storage 3. Formulary 4. Prescription 5. Dispensing 6. Administration of medicine 6. Monitoring of patients after medication administration 7. Obtaining medicines when the pharmacy is closed 8. Obtaining medicines, not in Hospital Formulary 9. Errors and adverse events 10. Narcotics and Psychotropic medicines 11. Chemotherapeutic agents, and 12. Implants and medical supplies.

Under each of the above headings, 'Dos' and Don'ts are explained, thus, if followed faithfully, a perfect pharmacy can be established and put to service. As the full text of the above NABH document is beyond the scope of this chapter, students and pharmacists are advised to refer to the same whenever they are assigned the duty or role of obtaining NABH accreditation for their hospital.

Questions

Short Answer Questions

1. Define hospital pharmacy.
2. Write briefly about the origin and development of hospital pharmacy.
3. Write a note on the responsibilities of a Hospital Pharmacist.

Long Answer Questions

4. Enumerate the organisational structure of a modern hospital pharmacy.
5. Explain the Job specifications of various sections of a hospital pharmacy.
6. Describe the works of a hospital pharmacy with qualified persons appointed to carry out those jobs.
7. What are the duties a pharmacist is expected to perform after dispensing in a modern hospital pharmacy set-up?
8. Explain the staff requirement, infrastructure and workload of a modern hospital pharmacy.
9. Write a note on Interprofessional relationships in a hospital
10. Write an essay about Good Pharmacy Practice in hospital
11. What are the standards prescribed for hospital pharmacy by FIP and ASHP?
12. Explain NQAS guidelines for hospital pharmacy.
13. Enumerate NABH Accreditation and the role of pharmacists in it.
14. Explain the staff requirement and infrastructure of a modern hospital pharmacy

CHAPTER 2

HOSPITAL COMMITTEES

Pharmacy and Therapeutic Committee

Introduction

A spurt in the growth of scientific knowledge and availability of sophisticated electronic instruments and equipment in the last few decades led to thousands of new drugs being introduced into the market. It is estimated that more than 70,000 formulations are available in India for prescribing by doctors. It is obviously impossible for anybody to remember so many formulations and their uses or merits.

Hence it is necessary for the hospital to establish a system to bring the best medicine to the attention of the staff, and this assists them in the proper selection of drugs for the treatment of patients. This educational programme is achieved through the 'Pharmacy and Therapeutic Committee' formed in the hospitals.

It is a committee of the medical and Paramedical staff and serves as a liaison between the medical staff and the pharmacy service on all matters pertaining to the use of drugs in the hospital.

Definition

Hassan defines Pharmacy and Therapeutic Committee as "a policy framing and recommending body to the medical staffs and the administration of the hospital, on matters related to the safe and rational use of drugs".

Objectives

There are three major roles for the Pharmacy and Therapeutic Committee:

1. Advisory
2. Education and
3. Safe and rational use of drugs

1. Advisory

   As seen earlier, the primary role of PTC is to assist the physician in the proper selection of drugs. Hence PTC is advising on the formulation and adaptation of policies regarding the evolution, selection and therapeutic use of drugs in hospitals. Thus, its main objective is to serve in an advisory capacity to the medical staff and hospital administration in all matters related to the use of drugs, including investigational drugs. It also advises the pharmacy department regarding effective drug distribution and control.

2. Education

   PTC helps the administration of hospitals in formulating programs to meet the educational needs of all the staff concerned, like Physicians, Nurses, Pharmacists and other healthcare professionals, to update their knowledge on matters related to drugs and their use. Towards this objective, PTC is entrusted with the function of selecting staff for the continuing education program and also preparation and updating of the Hospital formulary – a valuable reference book for hospital staff.

3. Safe and rational use of drugs

   As present-day medicines are highly potent and powerful, one has to take extra care while handling, administering and using the drugs. If the advice of PTC and its educational support are correctly followed, the safe use of drugs can be ensured. But in reality, medical staff, nurses and pharmacists overlook the guidelines given by the PTC, resulting in irrational and dangerous use of drugs. When an adverse incident involving the use of drugs happens and is reported outside, everybody starts blaming each other for whatever happened. Hence PTC is repeatedly warning the staff not to ignore its guidelines on matters pertaining to the safe and rational use of drugs. Thus, the first two objectives of advice and education are to achieve the final objective of the safe use of drugs.

Composition

The Composition of the committee may vary from hospital to hospital. However, the following composition is generally followed:

1. A minimum of 3 physicians from among the medical staff of the hospital.
2. A Pharmacist (usually the HOD or chief pharmacist)
3. A Nurse and
4. An Administrator

One among the above physician is appointed as the chairman of the committee. The pharmacist is designated as the secretary.

PTC also constitutes many sub-committees, which are either permanent or formed for a specific purpose temporarily. In these sub-committees, specialists are included either as presidents or as members in order to utilise their knowledge and experience in the particular field. Thus, there may be a sub-committee on Antibiotics, cardiovascular drugs, hormones and corticosteroids, narcotics and other CNS drugs.

PTC can also invite persons from within or outside the hospital to its meetings who can contribute their specialised knowledge and judgments. The committee must meet regularly at least six times a year, or more times if necessary. As it is usual with any committee, the secretary should maintain minutes of the meeting with all necessary other documents. The decisions of the committee are communicated to the people concerned and implemented or executed by the secretary. These works are reported by him to the committee members in the next committee meeting.

Primary Functions

Though PTC has advisory and educational objectives, the primary or ultimate aim of the PTC is the safe and rational use of drugs in the hospital. In order to fulfil that objective, PTC plays important role in the following:

1. Adverse Drug Reaction (ADR) monitoring
2. Drug product defect reporting
3. Psychotropic drugs use
4. Emergency drugs use
5. Drug utilisation review and
6. Safe use of all drugs.

Each of the above functions is meticulously carried out by PTC by issuing necessary regulations and guidelines to the staff concerned. Let us have a look at these guidelines in detail.

1. ***Adverse drug reaction monitoring (PTC and ADR):*** Adverse drug reaction is defined as a reaction that is noxious, unintended and occurs at *normal* doses used in humans. Though it occurs less frequently, the cause for it must be thoroughly investigated to prevent such reactions in other patients, or at least to be vigilant on all patients given the drug in question.

   Hence, some organisations in the hospital must be given charge of this responsibility. PTC takes up this responsibility and monitors the therapy throughout the hospital. Its main aim is to prevent ADR and, if occurred, to take follow-up action, including treatment to the particular patient, reporting to the authorities concerned, and avoiding such ADR in future.

In order to do that effectively, PTC issues a set of guidelines to the medical and Para-medical staff of the hospital, including the ADR reporting form, to report the unfortunate event of its occurrence without hiding.

On receipt of an ADR report from the department or ward where it occurred, PTC starts its investigation to find out the reason for that particular ADR. If necessary, it calls for further information from the reporting physician, nurse or patient. At the end of an investigation by its sub-committee specially assigned this duty, PTC submits its report to the authorities, whoever is concerned. Usually, it is reported first to the Dean or Director of the hospital and then to ADR reporting authority of the State and/or Central Government and to State Drugs Control Authorities. Depending upon the seriousness and frequency of this ADR, the drug in question may be withdrawn from the market on the orders of the Drugs Control Department or its issues a warning to the medical fraternity to be vigilant while using the particular drug through press or media.

2. ***Drug product defect reporting (PTC and drug defect):*** Though everybody is concerned with the use of drugs, especially patients and doctors, expect a zero error or 100% defect-free product, it is not always possible. Due to machine error or human error, occasionally, the drug reaches the user point with some or other noticeable defect. Such defects should be detected by the pharmacist or nurse, or doctor before it reaches the patient. If detected, they are duty bound to report the same to the PTC of the hospital.

   Reportable defects include inadequate packing, confusing or inadequate labels, deteriorated, contaminated or defective dosage forms, inaccurate fill or count of a drug product, defective drug delivering apparatus, etc. Obviously, the healthcare professionals should report anything which, in their professional opinion, is considered to be defective or undesirably associated with the drug product.

   PTC, on receipt of the above report, initiated an investigation and take possession of the suspected drug product from the reporter. It reports the matter, after verification, first to the manufacturer and then to other authorities concerned, if necessary. It also orders physical inspection of the entire lot or batch of the product supplied to the hospital and takes necessary action.

By this program, a sense of vigilance and duty consciousness is instilled in the minds of healthcare professionals, and ultimately patients are getting defect-free products.

3. ***Psychotropic drugs use (PTC and dangerous drugs):*** Psychotropic drugs are those drugs which, on longer use, produce dependence or addiction, and hence it, is dangerous to the patient as well as the society. Hence, they are also called dangerous drugs. PTC develops guidelines whereby dangerous drugs are purchased, stored, dispensed and properly administered under control.

   The procedure for this is no different from the Psychotropic Substances Acts and rules. PTC ensures strict adherence to the above Act by the hospital staff. In some hospitals, automatic stop orders are in force whereby "all drug orders for narcotics, sedatives and hypnotics shall be automatically discontinued after 48 hours, unless

   1. the order indicates the exact number of doses to be given
   2. an exact period of time for the medication is specified or
   3. the attending physician records the medication."
   4. In some other hospitals, the automatic stop orders require "all orders for narcotics, sedatives and hypnotics must be rewritten every 24 hours". Thus, the PTC takes care of the use of psychotropic drugs and the patients of the hospital.

4. ***Emergency drug use (PTC and emergency drugs):*** As the time factor is very important during emergency cases, PTC prepares a list of drugs and other supplies to be available in emergency boxes. These boxes are kept in all important places of the hospital and given charge to some pharmacists or nursing supervisors of the hospital.

   As these medicines are available literally by the side of the beds of emergency cases, they are also referred to as 'Bedside Pharmacy'.

   After the emergency cupboards have been placed on the wards and other places like the emergency procedures room of the department of radiology, it is mandatory that a program be developed whereby they are checked daily either by the hospital pharmacist or by the nursing supervisor responsible for the ward. The drug used on the day is replenished as early as possible so that a constant number of drugs are always available in the emergency cupboard.

   Usually, some 30 items of important, lifesaving drugs and about 10 to 15 items of surgical instruments and dressings, including syringes and needles, are kept in the emergency boxes. The list may vary depending on the need of a particular hospital which may decide to add or delete some items in the emergency box. Overall, the PTC of the hospital is responsible for the preparation and up-keeping of the emergency Drugs kit or 'Bedside Pharmacy'.

5. ***Drug utilisation review: (PTC and drugs use*):** Drug utilisation includes prescribing, dispensing and administering prescription drugs. Though there is no drug utilisation review outside a hospital, such a review can be organised in a hospital by PTC. Providing a "Hospital formulary" is one of the institutional authorities to control drug utilisation and a mechanism for continuing the education of physicians, nurses and pharmacists.

   Obtaining the 'Medication History' of the patient and maintaining the 'Patient medication profile' are the other two programs useful for a pharmacist to monitor drug utilisation within the hospital.

   Medication histories are taken by a clinical pharmacist of a required patient admitted to the hospital or seen in the outpatient department. This is accomplished by personal interview or through a computerised questionnaire specifically designed for the purpose and if the patient is in a condition to answer those questions.

   If not, the interview is conducted at the appropriate time, but at the earliest, with the help of the patient's helpers or family members. During the interview, details regarding medicines taken during the recent past, at the time of admission and OTC drugs are taken, if any, are collected.

   Also, information about known drug allergies, idiosyncrasies towards food products and about lab tests or anything conducted using diagnostic agents are also recorded. This information is passed on to the treating physician for early correct diagnosis and prescribing.

   The patient medication profile can be prepared and maintained by both hospital pharmacists and community pharmacists because drug utilisation review is not possible without the medication history of the patient. Community pharmacists can maintain the patient medication profile of the patients who frequent their pharmacy for getting medicines for themselves and their family members. Their services will be much useful in the case of patients requiring long-time therapy and those who continue treatment from their home as outpatients, such as diabetes, hypertension, asthma, epilepsy and TB patients.

   Modern community pharmacies, with graduate pharmacists and computer systems in their pharmacy, are offering such services to the patient.

6. ***PTC and safe use of drugs:*** Day by day, lots of new drugs are introduced by hundreds of pharmaceutical manufacturers throughout

the world. Consequently, the responsibilities of health care professionals in general, pharmacists in particular, also increased many folds. Possibility of error in prescription writing, dispensing and administration of these new drugs poses a great problem to the pharmacist, especially when the chances for Drug interaction, ADR and other problems are relatively unknown for the new drugs.

Hence PTC formulates many policies and guidelines to be followed by all concerned while handling not only new drugs but even the existing drugs. The following are some guidelines:

1. The hospital should appoint a qualified pharmacist to supervise the entire pharmacy services. He must be at least a graduate in pharmacy with adequate experience.
2. All dispensing operations must be carried out by qualified registered pharmacists. Non-pharmacy people should not be engaged in dispensing.
3. Adequate number of pharmacists must be appointed proportionate to the workload and round-the-clock service.
4. Hospitals must provide adequate and safe workspace and storage facilities for the pharmacy.
5. Hospitals should have a hospital formulary, and it should be updated every now and then or at least once in a year.
6. The pharmacist must follow all the rules regarding the storage and dispensing of narcotics, poison, and external use preparations.
7. In the hospital manufacturing section, the drugs should be manufactured according to Current Good Manufacturing Practices (CGMP) and other rules by the Drugs Control Department. Strict quality control and quality assurance measures must be followed.
8. All wards and Nursing stations should be periodically checked for expired drugs, deteriorated drugs, legibility of labels etc.
9. The pharmacy should have a small library with reference books on pharmacology, toxicology, posology and pharmacopoeia, hospital formulary, drug index, etc.
10. Periodical continuing education programs should be conducted by the hospital for the staff, and attendance for those programs must be compulsory.

If the above guidelines and any other guidelines issued from time to time by PTC are followed in letter and spirit, the safe use of drugs in the particular hospital can be ensured by and large.

Other Functions of PTC

1. The manufacturing unit of the hospital is inspected by the PTC for quality production.
2. PTC visits outside manufacturing units before approving their products for inclusion in the hospital formulary or purchase list.
3. Prepares written policies and procedures for the evaluation, selection, purchase, storage, dispensing and use of drugs.
4. Prepare the Hospital formulary and updates it periodically.
5. Forms sub-committees, as and when necessary, on the subjects considered essential by it.
6. Establishes procedures for cost-effective drug therapy.

Infection Control Committee

Members of this committee include epidemiologists, nurses and physicians from various clinical departments; others deemed appropriate by the chairperson of the committee can be included. The primary responsibility of the committee is to control infections spreading from the patient to the employees and others inside the hospital. The other responsibilities are:

1. To frame policies and procedures for isolation, outbreak investigation, surveillance and environment control.
2. To advise on products that have an impact on infection control.
3. To frame policies and monitor their implementation concerning the use of equipment, sterilisation and procedures.
4. To make recommendations to control the occurrence and spreading of infections.
5. To approve department-wise infection control policies and procedures and
6. To evaluate significant infections occurring in hospital employees.

Role of Pharmacists in Preventing Antimicrobial Resistance

A Pharmacist must monitor the patients those who are under antibiotic therapy. Abuse of antibiotics is the major reason for antimicrobial resistance; hence pharmacists must prevent non-compliance, at least by the patients under antibiotic therapy. There are different roles for the community pharmacist and the hospital pharmacist though both can counsel the patients.

A community pharmacist should not dispense less number of doses of antibiotics prescribed on any account. Even if the patient demands 3 or 4 antibiotic capsules or tablets citing lack of money in his hand pharmacist must politely refuse to dispense. He can either ask the patient to arrange money or reduce non-essential medicine, if any, in the prescription. If he explains the reason or rationale behind his refusal patiently, the patient will understand. Pharmacists should have that patience and responsibility in order to save the society he lives in from the danger of resistant microbes.

In hospitals, the pharmacist has different opportunities to work against antimicrobial resistance. In every hospital, the Antibiotics committee is constituted for the purpose. This committee is mainly formed to promote the rational and safe use of antibiotics in the hospital. Hence the responsibilities of it are:

1. Review of antibiotic prescriptions dispensed.
2. Regular periodic review of antibiotic usage.
3. Detect, enquire and supervise antibiotic-resistant cases.
4. Guide and advice on the products useful in infection control.
5. Carry out research on new antibiotic formulations.

Among the above, antibiotic resistance is considered critical and needs full attention by the committee because of its danger to society. In the antibiotic committee, a pharmacist can contribute significantly because he dispenses and monitor the use of antibiotics and hence is in a position to detect the noncompliance by the patients, which is one of the main reasons for antibiotic resistance. He can detect them through patient medication interviews as well as patient counselling, both of which are his primary functions as a clinical pharmacist. As antibiotic misuse is widespread, resulting in the danger of creating resistant strains of microorganisms, his role in controlling such a situation is very much important. Hence, he is given the role of secretary or coordinator of this committee.

Questions

Short Answer Questions

1. Define PTC.
2. What are the objectives of PTC?
3. Name the composition of members of PTC.
4. Write a note on PTC and emergency drugs.
5. What are the other functions of PTC?
6. Write the functions of the infection control committee of a hospital.

Long Answer Questions

1. Enumerate the functions of PTC.

2. Explain the role of PTC in the safe use of drugs.
3. Justify the need for forming PTC in hospitals.
4. How PTC controls ADR in hospitals?
5. Discuss the role of pharmacists in antimicrobial resistance.

CHAPTER 3

HOSPITAL FORMULARY

Introduction

The hospital formulary is nothing but the hospital's own pharmacopoeia. It differs from Pharmacopoeia, in that, it is a small size book, fits in apron pocket, so as to be suitable for on-the-spot reference and it has other useful information also, for the health care team especially trainees. Pharmacopoeia is published by the Government for the use of entire country, whereas, Hospital Formulary is published by a particular hospital to be used in that hospital only.

Objectives

The ultimate aim of publishing a hospital formulary is to give the best treatment to the patient at less cost. Hospital formulary as a book has the following objectives.

It provides information on the following:

1. The name and other details about the drugs approved by the Hospital (to be prescribed to the patients of the particular hospital).
2. Hospital policies and procedures on the use of the above drugs.
3. General Information such as dosing rules, abbreviations etc.

Development of Hospital Formulary

In order to develop a hospital formulary, one should know its content and guiding principles, hence they are given below.

Content

The contents of the formulary are arranged under three main sections:

Section 1: Introduction (Policies and Procedures)

Section 2: List of Drugs and

Section 3: Additional Information

Section 1: Introduction (Policies and Procedures)

In this section, detail about the Pharmacy and Therapeutic Committee, the name of its members and their designation and official addresses are given. Then the detail of the sub-committee or the special committee which prepared the formulary and duties and responsibilities given to the various members of the sub-committee are detailed. It is followed by the guidelines on how to use the formulary and the interpretation, meaning and legal limitations of its content. Reference to sources of detailed information on formulary drugs, such as Pharmacopoeias, National Formularies and the Hospital's own Drugs Information services, are given here.

As the formulary is binding in nature to the medical and paramedical staff of the hospital, it contains all the policies of the hospital with reference to the use of drugs. For example, it describes hospital regulations governing the prescribing, dispensing and administration of drugs. It also explains the rules regarding the prescription of controlled (narcotics) drugs, automatic stop orders, verbal drug orders, use of drug samples, reporting ADR and medication errors etc.

Pharmacy operating procedures, like working hours of various pharmacy wings of the hospital, outpatient services, inpatient services, pharmacy charging system, Drug information services etc., are also included in this premier of the hospital formulary so as to ensure a tussle-free, smooth functioning of the hospital.

Section 2: List of Drugs

This section is the heart of the formulary. It lists the entire range of drugs and formulations approved by the hospital for prescribing to the patients of the hospital. They can be arranged under any one of the following methods.

1. Drugs under generic names, arranged alphabetically.
2. Drugs are under generic names, arranged alphabetically but within the therapeutic classification.
3. Combination of the above two methods, in which the majority of the drugs are arranged under the first method, and a few therapeutic classes like ophthalmic drugs, otic drugs, dermatological preparations etc., are separately printed and drugs under the generic name listed alphabetically in each of the above special sections

As elaborate information about each drug is not possible and will defeat the very purpose of a book for ready reference, the formulary contains minimum essential information on each drug. They are:

1. Generic Name, if not available, as in the case of formulations, common name or even trade name.

2. Synonym, if any.
3. Dosage forms, strengths, packages and sizes commonly stocked in the hospital's pharmacy.
4. Formula, if it is a combination product.
5. Dose (adult, children and pediatric).
6. Special instructions/precautions.

Section 3: Additional Information

The hospital formulary is prepared to guide and help the entire healthcare team of the hospital. Hence it contains information useful for nurses, dieticians, Lab. technicians and other public health workers. The following is the wealth of information available in a hospital formulary:

1. Posology (including methods of calculating doses)
2. Pediatric doses
3. Poisons and antidotes
4. Important laboratory values
5. Nutrition and calorific values
6. Height and weight chart
7. Immunization schedule
8. Diagnostic and pathological reagents
9. List of hospital-approved abbreviations and
10. General and pharmacological index

Guiding Principles to Include or Exclude a Drug while Developing a Hospital Formulary

The very difficult task of the Pharmacy and Therapeutic committee is the selection of drugs to include in the formulary. This is more difficult because no member of the sub-committee formed for the purpose of preparation of the formulary is experienced enough in all the fields of therapy. Hence the committee always invites specialists from a particular field to its meetings to take a decision about the group of drugs used or available in the particular field. Thus the expert's, as well as the hospital staff's own experience, is the very first, undisputable guideline to include or exclude a particular drug in the formulary.

The second criterion is the inclusion of a particular drug or formulation in other standard books like Pharmacopoeias, National formularies etc.

The third one is that the manufacturer of a particular drug must have proven integrity, dependability and a track record.

The fourth one is that the product in question must be approved, accepted and in the market for a long time.

The fifth one is that the drug or formulation must declare all its content on the label, and no secret composition is acceptable to the committee.

The sixth principle is that the drug or formulation must comply with all legal requirements of the Drugs and Cosmetic Act and Rules, etc.

If the drug, after approval and inclusion in the formulary, is found to be deficient in any one of the above principles, it will be deleted from the formulary by suitable notification or circular by the PTC.

The above principles may be published in the hospital formulary itself and/or circulated among the staff of the hospital so as the staff to acquire an understanding of why a particular drug is not found or left out from the formulary. Also, it encourages staff concerned to recommend a particular drug to the PTC if it meets all the above guiding principles.

Preparation of the Formulary

PTC of the hospital, as and when it decided to prepare and adopt a formulary for the hospital concerned, constitutes a subcommittee for the purpose. The director or chief of pharmacy services of the hospital is given responsibility for preparing the formulary with the active participation and cooperation of all the members of the sub-committee.

The sub-committee is briefed on the series of rules or guidelines (refer above) to evaluate drugs for admission to the formulary and also on the content, format etc., by PTC. If the PTC decides to have only a drug list or catalogue for use in the hospital instead of a full formulary that is conveyed to the subcommittee, which prepares the one desired. However, there are many differences between a formulary and a mere drug list.

A formulary is more informative in nature, as described above, its contents range from generic names of the drugs to posology, poisons and antidotes, and data required by nurses, dieticians and lab technicians, whereas the drug list or catalogue contains only the name of the drug and dose range.

Thus the formulary has an informative, educative role and hence is useful to trainee doctors, nurses and pharmacists. However, the preparation, maintenance and updating of the drug's list or catalogue are easier compared to the formulary. Additions and deletions are easily made to the list, whereas it requires a lot of effort, time and cost to update a formulary.

Additional information, if any, required about a drug in the list can be obtained only by referring to suitable sources like books, manufacturer's literature or the internet or drug information centres. But the formulary gives adequate, essential information about each drug in a nutshell.

Format and Appearance

As the formulary is for ready reference on daily basis, its format is very important. Looking at the previously published formularies of another hospital within the country or abroad will give an idea to develop the one suitable for local conditions. Thus the formulary published by Vellore Christian Medical College (CMC) hospital in Tamil Nadu offers a very good model for others. The National formulary of India (NFI) published by the Government of India is equally useful as a forerunner.

Size: Experience has shown that a formulary which is sufficiently small in size to fit into the apron or clinical/lab coat will enjoy the acceptance of all concerned. Thus it can be in the size of or 10 cm × 18 cm.

Appearance: Each section of the formulary can be printed in different colour papers, thus helping the user to locate the particular section more quicker. Thus poisons and antidotes section, for example, can be printed on pink colour paper and a pediatric section on light green colour paper, laboratory values on blue colour paper and so on. Additionally, or alternatively, 'edge index' can also be used, but which makes the production cost to go up marginally.

Since the formulary is to be used often and carried daily, good bound volumes should be prepared with covers ranging from paper and cardboard to plastic or leather binding. At the same time, the formulary should be printed on good quality paper in order to reduce its overall weight to carry in coat packets easily.

Moreover, the hospital formulary must be updated and revised as often as possible or necessary. Usually, the formulary is updated once a year. In the meanwhile, if required, supplements may be published in between the editions.

The hospital formulary copies can be sent to the higher authorities like the Pharmacy Council of India, State Pharmacy Council, Director of Medical Education, Director of Medical and Public Health Services, Director of Drugs Control and the Library of the University of Health Sciences.

Advantages and Disadvantages of Hospital Formulary

Advantages

1. Patients are assured of safe and rational drug therapy.
2. The treatment given to them costs less compared to treatment with irrational and expensive drugs or drugs with doubtful benefits.

Disadvantages

1. It restricts doctors' freedom to prescribe drugs of their choice.

2. If the formulary is not updated regularly, new and effective drugs arrived cannot be prescribed to patients.
3. If the guiding principle for including or excluding a drug in the hospital formulary is not followed strictly, there are chances of unwanted drugs entering into the formulary or deserving drugs being left out of the formulary, which results in the defeating the very purpose of hospital formulary.

Nevertheless, by and large hospital formulary system is a most useful system for a large country like India.

Use of Hospital Formulary

These are given above as advantages of the Hospital formulary. That apart Hospital policies and procedures on the use of drugs are listed in Hospital's Formulary, and General Information, such as dosing rules, abbreviations, Lab values etc., are also given; hence they are very much useful to hospital staff.

Questions

Short Answer Questions

1. What is a Hospital formulary?
2. What are the objectives of the Hospital formulary?
3. Discuss the advantages and disadvantages of Hospital formulary.

Long Answer Questions

4. Explain the content of the Hospital formulary.
5. What are the criteria for selecting a drug to include in the Hospital formulary?
6. What are the guiding principles for preparing a Hospital formulary?
7. How do Hospital formularies differ from Pharmacopeia? Explain the format and appearance of the Hospital Formulary.

CHAPTER 4

SUPPLY CHAIN AND INVENTORY CONTROL

Preparation of Drugs List

In order to function effectively and without errors, a pharmacist needs to have certain basic knowledge about the drugs. For that, a few lists of drugs are essential so as to help him with as ready reference during the course of dispensing. They are the High-Risk drugs list, Emergency drugs list, Schedule H1 drugs list, NDPS drugs list and Reserved Antibiotics list.

High-Risk Drugs List

High-risk drugs are medicines that have an increased risk of causing significant harm to patients or even death if they are misused or used in error. They include,

= Drugs with a narrow therapeutic index

= Drugs that present a high risk when administered via the wrong route or other medicine management system error.

At the outset, one must be clear that there is no standard list of high-risk drugs. It is prepared largely based on the experience of incidents the health care team witnessed. They may vary between hospitals and other healthcare settings depending on the type of medicines used and the patients treated. In Australia, for example, the 'A PINCH' system of high-risk drugs list is in practice. [A PINCH is an acronym where each letter stands for the first letter of a particular group of drugs]

A. Antimicrobials include Aminoglycosides, Gentamicin, Tobramycin, Amikacin, Vancomycin, and Amphotericin –liposomal formulation.

P. Potassium and other electrolytes: Injections of concentrated electrolytes like Potassium, Magnesium, Calcium and Hypertonic Sodium Chloride

I. Insulins

N. Narcotics [opioids] and other sedatives, Morphine, Hydromorphone, Oxycodone, Fentanyl, Alfentanil, Remifentanil, and analgesic patches, Benzodiazepines, Diazepam, Midazolam, Thiopentone, Propofol and other short-term anaesthetics.

C. Chemotherapeutic agents: Vincristine, Methotrexate, Etoposide, Azathioprine oral chemotherapy

H. Heparin and other anticoagulants: Warfarin, Dabigatran, Riaroxaban, Apixaban.

Emergency Drugs

As the name implies, these are the drugs used in an emergency situations in hospitals and other places to save the life of the patient. Complications can occur and create an emergency at any time in critical cases admitted in wards. Hence these medicines are kept ready in nearby cub-boards in the wards and hence aptly called as 'bedside pharmacy' The **emergency drugs** are:

1. Aminophylline 0.25 gm/10 ml
2. Amphetamine sulphate 20 mg/ml
3. Amyl nitrite inhalation
4. Atropine sulphate 0.4 mg/ml
5. Caffeine sodium benzoate 0.5 gm/2 ml
6. Calcium gluconate 1 gm/10 ml
7. Chlorpheniramine maleate 10 mg/ml
8. Digoxin 0.25 mg/ml
9. Diphenyl hydantoin sodium 50 mg/ml
10. Epinephrine HCl 1:1000
11. Heparin 10,000 units/ml
12. Hydrocortisone 100 mg
13. Isoproterenol 1:100
14. Magnesium sulphate injection of 10% and 50%
15. Mannitol injection 25%
16. Nalorphine HCl 10 mg/2 ml
17. Neostigmine Methyl sulphate 0.25 mg/ml
18. Nor. epinephrine Injection 0.2%
19. Pentobarbital 50 mg/ml
20. Phenobarbital 120 mg/ml
21. Phenylephrine HCl 10 mg/ml
22. Picrotoxin injection 3 mg/ml

23. Procainamide 100 mg/ml
24. Protamine sulphate 10 mg/ml
25. Saline for injection 30 ml
26. Sodium molar Lactate solution
27. Water for injection 50 ml

Other Items

1. Syringes of all sizes – each 2
2. Needles of all sizes – each 2
3. Venous canulisation set
4. Oxygen catheters
5. Sterile suction catheters
6. Razor with blades
7. Sterile gelatine sponge
8. Resuscitation tube & cart
9. Oxygen equipment
10. Burn sheets and
11. Other surgical instruments like scissors, forceps etc.

This list is incomplete, few more drugs may be added to the list depending on the type of patients or diseases treated in the particular hospital.

Schedule H1 Drugs

Drugs and cosmetics rules have many schedules; among them, Schedule H is very important for a pharmacist because it deals with the drugs to be dispensed only when a prescription is presented. Schedule H has been there for a long time, but antibiotics, anti-TB drugs and habit-forming drugs have been moved from it to Schedule H1 now. At present, there are 46 drugs coming under schedule H1, which mainly comprises third and fourth-generation cephalosporins, carbapenems, newer fluoroquinolones and first- and second-line anti-tubercular drugs. They are given below:

Schedule H1

Alprazolam	Doripenam
Balofloxacin	Ertapenem
Buprenorphine	Ethambutol Hydrochloride
Capreomycin	Ethionamide
Cefdinir	Feropenam

Cefditoren
Cefepime
Cefetamet
Cefixime
Cefoperazone
Cefotaxime
Cefpirome
Cefpodoxime
Ceftazidime
Ceftibuten
Ceftizoxime
Ceftriaxone
Chlorodiazepoxide
Clofazimine
Codeine
Cycloserine
Diazepam
Diphenoxylate
Gemifloxacin
Imipenem
Isoniazide
Levofloxacin
Meropenem
Midazolam
Moxifloxacin
Nitrazepam
Pentazocine
Prulifloxacin
Pyrazinamide
Rifabutin
Rifampicin
Sodium Para-amino salicylate
Sparfloxacin
Thiacetazone
Tramadol
Zolpidem

Note: Preparations containing the above drug substances and their salts, excluding those intended for topical or external use (except ophthalmic and ear or nose preparations) containing above substances are also covered by this Schedule.

NDPS Drugs

Drugs coming under Narcotic Drugs and Psychotropic Substances act are referred to as NDPS drugs. They are habit-forming and hence issued strictly under prescription. Examples are Hydrocodone, Methadone, Hydromorphone, Meperidine, Oxycodone, Fentanyl, Tapentadol, Tramadol, Buprenorphine, Butorphanol, Morphine, Nalbuphine, Propoxyphene, Pentazocine, Leorphanol, Remifentanil, Sufentanil and oliceridine.

Reserved Antibiotics

Antibiotics are classified into three groups by World Health Organisation. They are Access, Watch and Reserve [AWaRe], taking into account the impact of different antibiotics and antibiotic classes on antimicrobial resistance to emphasise the importance of their appropriate use.

This group includes antibiotics that should be reserved for the treatment of antibiotic-resistant cases. They should be used for treatment as a 'last resort' option. The reserved antibiotics are: 1. Azetreonam 2. Carumonum 3. Cifiderocol 4. Ceftaroline-fosamil 5. Ceftaroline –fosamil 6. Ceftazidine/ Aibactum 7. Ceftobiprole- medocaril 8. Ceftalozane/ tazobactum 9. Colistin-IV 10. Colistin- oral 11. Dalbavancin 12. Dalfopristin/ quinupristin 13. Daptomycin 14. Eraocycline 15. Furopenum 16. Fosfomycin-IV 17. Lefamulin 20. Lineezolid 21. Meropenum/aorbactum 22. Minocycline-IV 23. Omadacycline 24. Oritaancin 25, Plazomicin 26. Polymixin B [IV] 27. Polymixin B [Oral] 28. Tedizolid 29. Telavancin and 30. Tigecycline

These antibiotics are generally belonging to the groups Fifth generation Cephalosporins, Polymixins, Glycopeptides, Tetracyclines, Penems and Carbapenems and Aminoglycosides.

Purchase and Inventory Control

Procedure for Drugs Purchase

Drugs purchase procedure starts with the decision of what to purchase, i.e., the selection of drugs. That is done by the institutional expert committee or the Drug purchase committee of the Government. They scrutinise the items in the list of essential Drugs, Surgical items, and list of previously purchased drugs, add new requirements, analyse the slow-moving, non-moving and outdated items, and arrive at a list of drugs and surgical items for long-term and short time use. Then the process of initiating tenders starts.

A tender process is a method of purchasing goods or services for an organisation by which prospective suppliers are requested to quote their minimum price at which they can supply goods or services within a stipulated time. After that time is over, the tender documents submitted are opened in front of those who have participated in the process, whoever quoted the least price and fulfil other tender conditions by the purchaser will be awarded the contract for supplying the required items or services for a particular period.

Tenders will be invited by advertising in the leading all-India-level newspapers, regional papers and tender bulletins. The tender notification may also be issued to all pharma manufacturers associations and pharma publications to increase the number of participants and competition. The tender document can also be referred to as a 'price quotation' in common terms for supplying drugs and other items. Bulk purchasers like Tamilnadu Medical Services Corporation [TNMSC] may undertake inspections of manufacturing facilities to check whether Good Manufacturing Practice [GMP] is followed by them and their ability, capacity and reliability for supplying required items. However, small-quantity purchasers like hospitals may not undertake such inspections.

E. Tenders

Electronic tendering is an advanced procurement process where the bidder or competitor has to submit the tender documents online well in advance before the prescribed time to avoid any delay or problem during the bid submission. Guidelines for e. procurement and e. tender processes are given in detail by the Government of India in their website. [https://e.procure.gov.in]. They act as a guide to all the procurement agencies and pharmacists, as well as whoever is involved in drug purchases on behalf of their organisation. As the government is the bulk and repeat purchaser, they have streamlined the procedure, and guidelines can be followed even by non-government institutions. Hence pharmacists are expected to be familiar with the purchase procedure.

Purchase and inventory control are very important operations of a hospital pharmacy. Both these works and the procedures vary with the size of the hospital, distance from the source of supply, storage facilities and turnover, and, of course, on cost. Usually, in a hospital, the HOD of the Hospital Pharmacy or Chief Pharmacist and a few other senior pharmacists are assigned these works, as they require expertise, experience and endurance to carry out and complete them successfully. However, a budding pharmacist is expected to know the theoretical aspects of it and may be required to apply it in practice or assist the seniors as and when required. Knowledge of purchase and inventory control is required even if a fresh pharmacist decides to open his own community pharmacy store. Hence students are advised to take training in this aspect also while undergoing training in hospitals, otherwise, it is difficult to get such training anywhere else.

Definitions

As the three words, 'purchase' ', inventory' and 'control' are to be used repeatedly in this chapter, it is better to define them first. According to W.E. Hassan,

'Purchase' is defined as an act of getting something by paying money or its equivalent or simply to obtain or buy something for a price.

'Inventory' is an itemised list of goods with their estimated worth, especially an annual account of stock taken in any business.

'Control' is defined as an act of exercising power over something.

Purchase or Procurement

Purchasing authorities: Once we decide to purchase something for an organisation, the first question asked is who should purchase or who has the authority to purchase. Then only other aspects like what, where, when and how to purchase arise.

There are two views on the authority to be designated for purchasing. One view is that all institutional purchases should be centralised, and a purchase officer should be appointed for the purpose. Another view is that drugs and other related items are speciality items which require technical skills, and hence its, the purchase should be assigned to a pharmacist. However, it all varies with the policies of the Government or management of the hospitals. For example, there is only one centralised agent at the state level for the purchase of drugs and other items for all the hospitals of the state in Tamilnadu (Tamilnadu Medical Services Corporation, Chennai). Some other Governments have similar or other arrangements, as it has many advantages like better control on inventory, bulk purchase and consequent large discounts and prevention of malpractices and corruption at various levels.

However, if there are purchases at institutional level and a purchase officer is appointed for the purpose, he is expected to work in collaboration with the Chief Pharmacist or HOD of the pharmacy services, each recognising the importance of the function of the other. In this system, the pharmacist provides the specification for the drugs to be purchased and have the authority to reject any article which may be below the standard and specifications so that the purchase officer is guided and assisted in his function. Thus, there may be either one of the above authorities available for purchasing drugs for a hospital.

(a) In small hospitals, the purchasing function may be looked after by the officer in charge of stores or the Hospital superintendent with the help of a storekeeper. As these officers are having this work as an additional duty and perform it along with their regular duties, they minimise the work and heavily depend on the storekeeper, who may be a pharmacist.

The following are the functions of a purchasing authority, whether he is a purchase officer or Pharmacist. First of all, he must collect the purchase request form, commonly called an indent, from the pharmacy. After its approval by higher authorities, a purchase order should be issued to suppliers. All the records and documents pertaining to purchase should be properly maintained; so that follow-up actions in case of delayed supply or discrepancy in supply can be verified in future. In order to get drugs at a lower or more economical price, competitive bidding must be arranged by those who are responsible for the purchase. Similarly, quotations for the required items can be obtained from various suppliers by sending the list of requirements with specifications.

(b) The role of pharmacists is very limited in purchasing drugs in Indian hospitals as we employ only D. Pharm holders as pharmacists who are being easily dominated, and a full department of pharmacy services with graduate and postgraduate pharmacists is yet to be established in our hospitals. However, a pharmacist is supposed to know his future role in drug procurement. There is some pre-requisite before purchasing drugs for the hospital. Obviously, purchases cannot be made overnight. The role of the Pharmacist begins with the preparation of list of manufacturers, wholesalers or their local representatives with their addresses and phone numbers. He should keep ready the specifications for the drugs he indents to purchase. Then only he can prepare the purchase-request form or indent and send it to the purchasing authority. After his approval, drugs can be purchased from various sources depending on quantity and management's policy. The following are the suppliers of drugs to hospitals.

1. Manufacturers of drugs
2. Wholesalers
3. Retailers (in case of emergency)
4. Tender winners and
5. Contract suppliers

The pharmacist is required to inform the about these sources to the purchase officer, and the choice of supplier is either made by the pharmacist or left to the discretion of the purchase officer. Whatever may be the way of purchase of drugs, the pharmacist and authorities should make arrangements for testing the quality and standards of the drugs supplied to the hospital. It can be tested in the hospital's own testing lab, if available, otherwise, the samples can be sent to commercial testing laboratories or Government laboratories, and an order for purchase may be executed depending on the analytical report of the samples received. After the goods are received, the pharmacist should acknowledge it in the proper format, and if any item is returned to the supplier for whatever reason, he should prepare and submit a return goods memo and send it to the purchasing authority. The same procedure can be repeated after all the drugs are supplied and tested randomly for quality, and then the payment for the same is recommended to the hospital management.

In order to perform the above duties, especially for preparing specifications-pharmacist should use the books of standards like IP, BP, USP, National formulary, Pharmaceutical Codex etc.

Purchase Procedure

There are two procedures for the purchase of drugs, one is purchase through tenders, and another is an institutional method where many preliminary steps have to be followed, even if it is also through a tender process. They are explained below.

The initiation for the purchase of drugs starts with the pharmacists. After determining the drugs, their specifications, price, required quantity etc., the pharmacist should prepare a purchase request form. This form will have all the details mentioned above in addition to the available balance, anticipated monthly use etc. The original copy of this form is sent to the administrative officer in charge for the department, and upon his approval, it is forwarded to the purchasing department. A duplicate copy is maintained in the pharmacy department.

On receiving the purchase request form, the purchase officer prepares the purchase order in multiple copies, which will contain all the specifications, quantity etc., taken from the request form. First copy of the purchase order is sent to the manufacturer or supplier or his representative. The second copy is the accounts payable copy and is sent to the accounts department and kept in the file until goods are supplied, and the received report comes from initiating department. The third copy is retained by the purchase officer himself for his records and follow-up. The fourth copy is sent to the initiating department, i.e., the pharmacy. On receiving this copy pharmacist should check it with his purchase request form for accuracy or modifications.

Fifth and sixth copies are sent to the goods receiving department, which in turn verifies the goods and sent their received report to the accounts department in the fifth copy. If the goods are to be ordered again, the sixth copy can be used or ignored.

If some goods are returned to the supplier for some or other reason, a return goods memo is prepared in multiple copies and sent to initiating department, purchase officer, accounts department and stores.

Immediately after the goods are received, they are promptly entered in the purchase record, and stock registers with all the relevant details, like, invoice number and date, name of the supplier, quantity received etc.

Whenever an item is not supplied and is out of stock in the pharmacy and stores, an out-of-stock form should be prepared in duplicate and sent to initiating or consuming department so that a false sense of heavy demand is not created.

Control on Purchases

Almost all the superior authorities or managements of the hospitals attempt to limit the purchase volume by placing an upper limit in rupees terms on the purchase order. This method may not serve the purpose, as it is easily circumvented by issuing multiple small orders or results in fewer items and quantities, causing a shortage of drugs in the hospitals.

Inventory Turn Over

A more scientific method of control on purchases is to calculate the inventory turnover and order the goods accordingly. It is calculated by dividing the cost of goods sold or issued during the financial year by the average of opening and closing inventory costs. This gives the number of times the inventory has been turned over during the period.

For example, if the total cost of goods sold or issued in one year in a big hospital is Rs. 20 Lakhs and the opening inventory cost is Rs. 6 Lakhs, and the closing inventory cost is Rs. 4 Lakhs, then the average of them is calculated to be Rs. 5 Lakhs. On dividing the total cost of Rs. 20 Lakhs by this average gives a turnover rate of 4.

Inventory turnover of 4 times a year indicates the purchase was carried out properly in the previous year. That is, goods are purchased on an average of three months once, and it is considered as a satisfactory practice in the trade. This turnover rate can be up to 6, meaning thereby the purchase of goods once in 2 months if the organisation is running short of finance. But if it is more than 6, it denotes a pessimistic attitude of management and losing bulk purchase discounts. Pharmaceutical manufacturers are offering more incentives on bulk purchases, for example, if you purchase 10 bottles of cough syrup, they give one bottle free, at the same time, if you purchase 25 bottles, three bottles are given free, similarly for 50, ten bottles and for 100 twenty-five bottles are offered, thus decreasing your cost of purchase by 10% to 25% [or increasing your profit margin from 10% to 25%]. Moreover, repeated purchases of the same item many times in a year involve the cost of purchase every time and a waste of time and energy in the process of purchase.

On the other hand, a low turnover rate [less than 4] indicates duplication of stock, large purchases of slow-moving items and dead stock and investment.

Thus, purchases should be controlled in an efficient and reasonable manner. In order to do that, the purchasing authorities must know important aspects of inventory control; hence they are discussed below:

Inventory Control

While inventory is defined as an itemised list of goods with their estimated worth or value, inventory control is defined as a process of safeguarding the company's inventory and maintaining it at an optimum level.

The importance and uses of inventory control are listed below:

1. It reduces the cost of production
2. It minimises time wastage due to a shortage of raw materials
3. It minimises the wastage of goods
4. It minimises the capital investment
5. It maximises customer service
6. It helps to deliver the goods at the right place and at the right time.
7. The value of goods on storage can be seen at any time, and
8. It improves the overall handling and storing of goods.

Inventory Levels

While stocking goods, the inventory level should be optimum. Excess of stock leads to the huge cost of running the organisation, at the same time, less stock leads to many problems in the supply of required items at the required time. Hence store keepers follow some levels of stock, and they are,

1. ***Maximum level:*** A level is fixed after studying various factors; beyond which materials should not be purchased at any time, that level is called the maximum level.
2. ***Minimum level:*** It is a level beyond which the materials should not be allowed to fall at any time.
3. ***Re-order level:*** This is the level at which an order should be placed to replenish the stock.

Methods

Following are the various method of inventory control:

1. ***Periodic inventory control*:** In this method, a physical count of inventory at the end of each accounting period (a year) is undertaken.
2. ***Perpetual inventory control*:** In this method, entries are made in the register as and when the sale or issue is completed. Day-to-day entries thus made keep the record updated always. This is the method of inventory control followed in all the dispensaries and medical stores of the hospital, as an item or medicine going out of stock without knowing will create a lot of trouble and problems for the hospital.

3. ***Special inventory -Inventory for perishable drugs*:** Important lifesaving drugs like biologicals (antibiotics, vaccine, serum etc.) which undergo degradation easily and have short shelf-life should have special care. The following methods can achieve this:
   (a) Maintaining separate records for these items with their name, potency and expiry date.
   (b) Replacing the items nearing expiry or expired with a new ones by constantly checking the record as well as physical stock.

Control of Inventory

Hospital pharmacists must control the inventory by using various measures or parameters available for the purpose. They are EOQ (Economic Order Quantity) and RQL (Re-order Quantity Level). These measures can also be used to control the purchase volume.

***RQL*:** The greatest dilemma for a pharmacist during his professional practice in a medical store (of hospital or outside) is when and how much of an item of medicine should be ordered. An arbitrary decision on these aspects will definitely lead to trouble and loss; hence a scientific method is needed based on which a rational decision can be made by the pharmacist.

One of the methods to determine the time of order placing is RQL (Re-order Quantity Level). It is the level that must be reached before additional stocks are ordered. Sapp, *et al.* have developed a table to use EOQ and RQL, according to which, for determining the Re-order quantity, the average usage rate per month in units of issue should be divided by 13 weeks. Then multiply the figure by the average Vendor Lead Time (VLT) plus the safety factor. The following table illustrates the point:

VLT	Safety factor
0 to 2 weeks	1.0
2 to 5 weeks	1.5
5 to 8 weeks	2.0
8 to 11 weeks	2.5
11 to 15 weeks	3.0

$$\text{R.Q} = \frac{\text{Average usage rate per month}}{13} = \text{A}$$

$$= \text{A} \times (\text{VLT} + \text{SF})$$

Simpler Method of getting RQL is by multiplying lead time in days by the average daily usage of inventory. For example, if you are selling or dispensing on an average 20 bottles of B. Complex syrup per day and it requires seven days for the supplier to deliver the goods, then you must order for it when your stock reaches 140 [20 x 7] bottles.

EOQ (Economic Order Quantity): How much of an item is to be ordered is determined by using the EOQ factor. To calculate this factor, it is important to ascertain the cost of ordering and the cost of carrying the inventory or holding cost. Then the EOQ is calculated by applying the following formula:

$$\text{EOQ} = \frac{\sqrt{2 \times 12 \times \text{monthly usage} \times \text{cost of ordering}}}{\text{Unit cost} \times \text{Holding cost}}$$

It may be advantageous to order expensive items on a monthly basis and inexpensive items annually. Another method of calculating the EOQ is by mathematical approach. Here the formula used is,

$$\text{EOQ} = \sqrt{\frac{2AB}{C}}$$

Where,

A is the Annual usage of inventory in units

B is Buying cost per order

C is Carrying cost per unit

Example: If A = 1600 units, B = 50 Rs and C = 1Re, then

$$\text{EOQ} = \sqrt{\frac{2 \times 1600 \times 50}{1}} = \sqrt{160000} = 400 \text{ units}$$

However, in this method, there are some limitations, they are,

1. The sale per year is an assumption.
2. Time taken for supply is not considered.
3. If there is unexpected demand, this calculation is useless and
4. The EOQ calculated as above may be in fraction.

Nevertheless, instead of arbitrarily determining these quantities without any basis, it is better to use some scientific calculations. A pharmacist will learn these and other skills with his experience in the job. Majority of the times, calculations made using the discretion and the experience of a pharmacist will be correct and rewarding.

Maintaining Cold Storage

Though all the storage conditions for the drugs are essential and should be followed sincerely, cold storage acquires importance because of the unique characteristics of drugs stored in that condition. For example, biological drugs like vaccines, sera and antibiotics easily deteriorate if improperly stored without following storage conditions specified for them. Oral polio vaccine, for an instant, requires cold condition throughout its journey or transport from manufacturer to wholesalers to retailers to Hospitals and until it is administered to the patient. This continuous cold storage is referred to as a cold chain arrangement. A Pharmacist must ensure this cold chain without any interruption at any point.

In order to store the drugs under cold conditions, various devices are used. They are Refrigerators, ILR, walk-in cold rooms etc. Among these devices, the Refrigerator is commonly used everywhere, and it has a thermostat control to set the cold temperature required. It is always maintained in good working conditions in all the drug stores, and a backup arrangement is provided in the case of a power failure for a long time. A number of Refrigerators are used in big drug stores to store the entire quantity of all the drugs requiring cold storage. They are periodically checked for proper working and for verifying the set temperature.

ILR Point or Cold Chain Point

An ILR Point or Cold Chain Point (CCP) is located at the health centre (Usually PHC/UHC/CHC) with an Ice Lined Refrigerator (ILR) for the storage of vaccines and a deep freezer for the preparation of frozen ice packs. The Cold Chain Point must have a generator as a power pack-up. It always maintains the temperature between + 2°C and +8°C.

Precautions for Storing Vaccines in an ILR:

1. Keep all the vaccines in the basket hanging in the ILR Box
2. No vaccine or diluent should be kept directly at the bottom of the ILR
3. Leave at least a 2 cm gap between boxes of vaccines for cold air circulation
4. A thermometer should be kept inside to monitor the temperature.
5. Freeze-sensitive and short-expiry vaccines should be stored at the top of the box, others at the bottom.
6. The time taken for the ILR to rise from +4° C to +8° C in the case of power failure is known as 'Hold Over Time'(HOT). It depends on many factors, but the normal HOT for an ILR is 20 Hours at 43° C
7. Vaccines should not be stored in domestic Refrigerators in the area where power failures are frequent and for a longer time. The HOT for domestic refrigerators is only for 4 hours, beyond which the vaccines and other drugs start deteriorating. Hence pharmacists should not switch off their refrigerators at night to save on electric bills, as practised by some pharmacists.

Walk-in Cold Rooms

According to UNICEF, 'Walk-in cold rooms and walk-in freezer rooms are refrigerator enclosures accessible via at least one door and large enough for a person to walk into, housed within existing buildings. The temperature inside the walk-in rooms will be around 0°C to 5°C. The Hold Over Time (HOT) for these rooms are 18 & 26 hours at 42°C and 32°C, respectively, if not opened.

FEFO and FIFO Methods of Storage

FEFO and FIFO are acronyms that stand for First Expire, First out and First in, First out, respectively. In the FEFO method expiry date of the goods (Drugs) that arrived in the store is noted, and the short-expiry items will be kept in the first row of the stores and sold or utilized first. In the FIFO method, goods arrive first in the store is sent out first, here, obviously, only the time of arrival is taken into account.

Which one among the two is the best?

In the FEFO method, importance is given to the expiry date of the goods, not the arrival time. Just because of some goods arrive later (but have very short self-life) and cannot be sold or used later as in the FIFO method. While storing drugs, pharmacists should give priority only to the expiry date, and he need not give importance to the time of arrival of drugs. First, in-First out method may be suitable for items without expiry date as items that came first to the warehouse may be getting old or deteriorating or gathering dust or getting an old stock appearance. Hence these factors play a major role in the FIFO method. Now a days, educated customers started looking at even manufacturing dates, though the expiry date is not prescribed for those items. They demand fresh stocks from the shop or store.

Hence a pharmacist must be vigilant while receiving stock and note both the manufacturing date and expiry date, and try to sell or use the items according to his judgement, intelligence and smartness.

Expiry Drugs Removal, Handling and Disposal

This author has a decade of experience in handling drug stores and used the following method for handling drugs with expiry dates and recommends it to pharmacy students. As and when drugs arrive in the store, each and every item's expiry date is noted in a diary or note, not one below another on a single page, but on the pages of a particular month. For example, if two drugs arrive, one with an expiry in the month of Sep 2023 and another with an expiry in Dec 2023, their name and quantity are written on the respective month page of a Diary or Notebook. Thus, the full month-wise expiry items list will be automatically ready in due course of time without physically verifying a large number of times and missing some items in that process. Now a days it is easy to do the same using a computer, thus a month wise list of expiry dates for drugs can be obtained while receiving the stock itself.

Then short, expiry items are sold or used first and when it is over, cut from the list. In hospital pharmacy stores, pharmacists should note the short-expiry items periodically and intimate the doctors of the hospital through their management. Thus, they are used as early as possible without allowing them to expire and thereby causing loss to the organisation. Alternatively, those short-expiry items are returned to the supplier to get the fresh stock in lieu of those drugs. Each manufacturer or supplier has a set of conditions for returning short-expiry items, like returning two months or three months before expiry etc... Those conditions should be followed by pharmacists to avoid disputes with them. Thus, a pharmacist has to be vigilant always and should make it a habit to verify drugs for expiry date at a fixed time interval, say once in a fortnight, month etc. Apart from random checking of a few items daily, whenever customers are not visiting the stores, it is also welcome.

Expired items, if not returned or accepted by the supplier, may be destroyed after informing and getting permission from management. While disposing of by destruction, care should be taken that they are fully destroyed without any chance of misuse or recycling. Hence the disposal should be under the personal supervision of pharmacist. This is especially true in the case of disposal of cytotoxic drugs and narcotics, which require prior information to the Drugs Inspector concerned or other authorities.

Documentation

There are many documents a pharmacist should prepare, update and keep ready for purchase and storage. They are all explained in the text of this chapter dealing with those topics. In brief, they can be listed as follows.

Purchase Department:

1. List of drugs to be purchased with specification, Quantity etc.
2. The purchase request form (Indent)
3. Purchase order (with multiple copies on different colour paper)
4. Return goods memo/Register
5. Purchase Record
6. Stock Register
7. Invoice file
8. Out-of-stock forms
9. Copy of Bill payment details by account dept.

Inventory /Stores Department:

1. Stock Register (general)
2. Stock Register for Narcotic drugs
3. Stock Register for Surgical Items
4. Record of drug's expiry dates and
5. Indent files (From Wards, Dispensary etc.)

Questions

Short Answer Questions

1. What is inventory control?
2. What are different inventory levels?
3. What are the different methods of inventory control?
4. What is the inventory turnover rate? How is it calculated?
5. What is RQL?
6. What is EOQ?
7. What is e. tender?
8. Write a note on Emergency drugs.
9. What are Reserved Antibiotics? Give examples
10. What are FEFO and FIFO methods of storage?
11. Which one among the FEFO and FIFO is the best?

Long Answers Questions

12. Explain the drug purchase procedure of a hospital. Enumerate the role of pharmacists in it.
13. How is inventory controlled in a hospital? Explain various methods and calculations involved.
14. How is purchase controlled in a hospital or medical store? Discuss the effect of excess or fewer purchase quantities.
15. Enumerate the role of purchasing authorities in purchasing drugs for a hospital.
16. Explain the e. procurement process.
17. Write a note on Expiry Drugs Removal, Handling and Disposal:
18. Explain ILR Point or Cold Chain Point
19. Enumerate the Precautions for Storing Vaccines in an ILR:

CHAPTER 5

MANAGEMENT OF CENTRAL DRUG STORE AND STORAGE OF DRUGS

Introduction

"Store is a place where physical storage of materials is made which are carried into the place in a scientific and systematic manner in order to save them from all kinds of damages and losses and exercising overall control on their movement". The act of organising and managing a store is known as storekeeping.

Almost all organisations have one or more stores in their premises, for example, there are raw material stores and packing material stores and finished product stores in the case of manufacturing companies, saleable goods in the case of shops, or at least records and reports in the case of the organisation not dealing with physical inventory. Thus, storekeeping has become a universal function which everybody must know, pharmacists are not an exemption.

Importance of Store Keeping or Warehousing

Materials pilferage, deterioration and careless handling leading to reduced profits or even losses for an organisation. It is more serious and important in the case of drugs and pharmaceuticals, where improper storage practices lead not only to lose in terms of money but also in terms of human lives. Hence, studying drug store keeping and management is very important for a pharmacist.

Types of Stores

There are three main types of stores:

1. Central stores where centralised buying and handling of drugs are undertaken.

2. Central stores with sub-stores: Here, buying is through central stores, but handling will be through many sub-stores.
3. Decentralized (or) Individual stores: Here, buying and handling of drugs are undertaken by the buyer and storekeeper of each department.

The type of stores adopted depends upon the circumstances prevailing in a hospital. Generally, the first or second type of stores is common. In the first type (central stores) there are a few advantages.

1. The labour required for this storage is less compared to decentralised storage.
2. Maintenance of a number of records is less in this method.

However, the main disadvantage is that this store may not be under the control of a qualified person. By appointing one or two assistant storekeepers with the required qualification, we can solve this problem to a greater extent.

In the decentralised method of storage, the main advantage is that it is under the control of a qualified person (pharmacist). He can adjust the inventory based on the prescribing trends, and that is another advantage of this method of storage.

Organization of Drug Store

In order to organise a drug store in a hospital, the following points should be considered:

(a) Location and layout

(b) Design of stores building and

(c) Management.

(a) Location and layout

The normal practice is to locate the drug store near the consuming department, that is, near the outpatient dispensary and wards. The important points to keep in mind regarding the location of stores are:

- Easy movement of materials.
- Good housekeeping.
- Sufficient space for men and material handling.
- Optimum use of storage space like floor, racks, shelves etc.
- Proper preservation from rain, sunlight and animals.
- The volume and variety of goods to be handled.
- Accessibility to modes of transportation such as lorry, van etc.

(b) Design of stores building

(i) Building: The store's building must have adequate facilities for the preservation of drugs. Facilities such as cold storage, air conditioning and similar facilities may be provided. The building must be strong, spacious, high enough, well ventilated and neatly arranged. The floor must be strong to withstand the pressure of frequent movement of materials.

(ii) Lighting: Clear and adequate lighting is essential at the same time, windows are kept to a minimum. Proper generator facilities should be provided in case of power failure, both for lighting and cold storage facilities.

(iii) Safety: The ways inside the stores must be kept clean and free from obstructions or materials, so that movement inside the stores is not affected or results in accidents. Provision of firefighting facilities is necessary for important places, especially where inflammable materials like chloroform, ether etc., are stored and handled. The entry of unauthorised staff and persons should be strictly prohibited, and the drug store should be kept under proper lock, wherever necessary.

(c) Management

Types of Materials Stored

1. Tablets
2. Capsules
3. Injections
4. Ointments, pastes and creams
5. Liquid orals, and
6. Chemicals

If not stored separately in a surgical store of the hospital, the following materials are also stored in the medical/drug store of the hospital under the control of a pharmacist.

- Bed sheets/blankets
- Bedside tables
- Cot
- LVP stands (saline stands)
- Needles
- Medical gases
- Syringes

- Surgical gloves
- Surgical dressings like bandages, gauze, cotton etc.
- Surgical equipment and instruments like scissors, forceps etc.
- Surgical suture and ligatures
- Trollies
- Wheelchairs etc.

Store Room Arrangement

Store rooms can be arranged under various techniques like alphabetically, pharmacologically, supplier-wise, formulation-wise, etc. Each of these methods has its own advantages and disadvantages. Usually, in a big store like a hospital store, the formulation-wise arrangement is followed. Thus, the drugs are arranged as follows:

1. Capsules
2. Chemicals
3. External use preparations
4. Injections
5. Liquid orals and
6. Tablets

Each one of these formulations is arranged alphabetically within their respective area of storage for easy location and issue. Moreover, there should always be adequate extra space for shelves to introduce, as and when required, in each of these areas. Thus, keeping one type of formulation - say tablets - in different places of the store can be avoided.

Category Wise Storage of Inventory

There are many ways of exercising control over the inventory. For example, drugs can be stored according to their cost, supply source or utility. As mentioned above, each method of storage has its merits and demerits, and hence a storekeeper has to decide which method is more convenient and suitable for him and his organisation. The inventory is analysed for its cost, source or utility, and those methods are referred to as ABC analysis, GOLF analysis and VED analysis, respectively.

ABC analysis: Here, the drugs are grouped according to the cost of the material as shown below:

'A' group items: This includes costly items such as biological and antibiotics. These items may not be more than 10% of the total inventory, but it consumes 70% of the total inventory cost.

'B' group items: These groups of items are neither costly nor cheap. They usually represent 20% of the total inventory, and the total investment on these items also does not exceed 20%.

'C' group items: These items are less expensive items but occupy 70% of the total stock, and the total cost does not exceed 10%.

Disadvantages of ABC analysis: Very critical and essential items for production or distribution may be included in the C category because they may not be costlier, i.e., very cheap. For example, magnesium stearate or talc in the manufacture of tablets, needles or plasters in the case of surgical items, and water for injections in the case of drugs, are cheaper compared to other items in these categories, but if they are not available, as a result of less attention and control being paid to the cheaper items, there may be a huge problem in the manufacture, operation or treatment respectively.

GOLF analysis: Here, the drugs are grouped depending upon the source of supply of the drug. Thus,

G - Government controlled items

O - Open market items

L - Local purchase items and

F - Foreign items, are stored according to this order

This is an arbitrary method of classifying the drugs, may not always be possible for a storekeeper to classify drugs according to this category. Hence, it is not followed much.

VED analysis: Here, the drugs are classified based on their utility.

V - Vital items

E - Essential items and

D - Desirable items

Vital items are very important items like lifesaving drugs without which a hospital cannot run. Essential items are a little less important than vital items, however, they are always available. Desirable items are not important compared to the first two categories; however, if it is available, it is welcomed, and at the same time, non-availability does not cause big problems. Some stores are arranged according to this method.

Storage of Drugs

Management of a Drug Store

1. Manpower: To manage a drug store, the first requirement is manpower. In order to fulfil the organisation of drug stores in a hospital, first, the qualified staff-- the pharmacists – must be

appointed in adequate numbers to manage and maintain the store. In addition to pharmacists, a sufficient number of clerical staff and labourers should be appointed to maintain accounts and to physically handle the materials, respectively.

2. Orderly arrangement: As mentioned earlier, drugs can be arranged on the shelves either alphabetically, pharmacologically or in formulations wise, like capsules, tablets, injections etc., whichever method is followed, the drugs should be easily traceable for issuing instantly.

The costly items must be kept under lock and key, similar to narcotic drugs. The heavy materials must be stored near the entrance or exit for obvious reasons. Vaccines, sera, suppositories and similar substances which require cold storage should be stored in refrigerators.

Markings on the Inventory

In order to locate, identify and know a few details about a particular item, some markings are made either on the product or on the place where it is stored. Thus, there are floor markings, shelf stripping and Goods markings for the above purposes.

Floor markings: In the wooden floor or concrete floor of the stores, the name of the item stored in the particular area is marked by paint.

Shelf stripping: Paper, card, plastic or metallic strips are used for shelf stripping in which the name of the item is written. Hence, the name of the item is more clearly visible, and the identification and location of them are easier.

The advantages of these types of markings are:

1. A particular area is allotted for a particular product
2. It brings orderliness and
3. It is easy to check the stock

Goods marking: In this method date of receipt of goods, cost price and supplier name are marked near or on the goods. Cost price is marked in code words; thus, it is easy to determine the discount while selling. Similarly, if different suppliers are there for a single product, goods marking helps in easy identification of the source of supply.

Card system: All the stored items are entered in separate cards, with their name, manufacturer, supplier, invoice no. and date, batch number, quantity, expiry date and any other details needed to refer to the particular item. Receipts and Issues are then and there entered on the card so that up-to-date information is available about that item. This card must be kept near or on the item. In these days of computerised inventory, this may be an outdated method of inventory control, however, still many hospitals are following this system, even to serve as a double check.

Stock checking: The hospital can assign the duty of checking the stock of drugs physically to certain people, and they should perform their duty with or without notice to the employees of stores. The closing balance on the stock card must tally with the actual balance. Damaged or expired drugs should be disposed of after necessary sanctions from the authorities.

Records: Every store should maintain a record of its purchase, issue and stock of drugs. All these entries in their register should have supportive documents like invoices, indents and other documents. They should be maintained up to date.

Thus a store should be managed by the pharmacist in a professional and efficient manner. The efficiency of drugs store management reflects in the following aspects:

1. It must be able to purchase quality drugs at a minimum cost.
2. It should scientifically store, maintain and preserve the drugs.
3. There should not be any interruption of the drug supply.
4. Suppliers should be promptly paid, and there should not be any complaints from them like delayed payment or part payment etc.
5. All facilities to prevent theft, pilferage, damage, or fire accident must be available.
6. Physical verification of stocks for expiry dates and stability must be undertaken as often as possible.

Storage Conditions

Storage conditions stipulated in each product must be adhered to maintain its safety and potency. Hence a store pharmacist must be thorough with the storage conditions of drugs. General statements like protect from sunlight, protect from moisture etc., should be followed and not ignored. Some products may require storage at specific conditions and the temperature that must be followed, storing either at lower temperatures or higher temperatures leads to unwanted problems. The storage conditions, even though given in general terms, are defined in all pharmacopoeias, including Indian pharmacopoeia. They are

(a) Cold: Any temperature not exceeding 8 °C and usually between 2 °C to 8 °C

(b) Cool: Any temperature between 8 °C to 25 °C

(c) Room temperature: The temperature prevailing in a working area (25 °C to 30 °C)

(d) Warm: Any temperature between 30 °C to 40 °C

(e) Excessive heat: Any temperature above 40 °C

(f) Protect from freezing: Freezing results in loss of strength or change in characters of the drug, in addition to the risk of breaking the container, hence, it must be carefully avoided.

(g) If no specific condition is given, it is understood as protection from light, moisture, freezing and excessive heat.

Questions

Short Answer Questions

1. List the types of stores
2. What is ABC analysis?
3. What is GOLF analysis?
4. What is VED analysis?
5. Write a note on marking the inventory.

Long Answer Questions

6. How is a drugstore organised?
7. How is a drugstore managed?
8. Explain category-wise storage of inventory. Discuss its advantages and disadvantages.
9. Write in detail about the storage of drugs. Add a note on the storage conditions of drugs.

CHAPTER 6

DRUGS DISTRIBUTION

Introduction

The drug distribution system in hospitals can be broadly classified into two. They are,

1. Distribution to outpatients or ambulatory patients.
2. Distribution to inpatients or institutionalised patients.

An outpatient or ambulatory patient is one who, after consultation and diagnosis, receives treatment which could be even for further diagnosis without being admitted to the hospital and does not require bed or hospitalisation. On the other hand, one who needs hospitalisation for treatment is admitted and given a bed in the hospital is known as an inpatient. Generally, the diseases of outpatients are such a nature that they require not more than a few days of treatment with some exceptions like diabetes, TB and asthma, whereas the inpatient's problems are complex and serious and may require close supervision, observation and treatment for a comparatively long time. Hence these categories of patients are admitted to the wards.

Distribution to Outpatients

As the distribution of drugs to outpatients is not complex compared to inpatients, in almost all the types of hospitals same system is followed. After consultation and diagnosis are over, patients are given a prescription (and small chits in which the Patient's hospital Number, name of the medicines prescribed and the quantity are written by the doctor). Then the patients or their helpers take the prescription to the dispensary or pharmacy situated near the main entrance of the hospital so that they can collect their medicine which is usually the final work for them in a hospital, and easily moves out of the hospital.

The drugs are issued to the patients through two or more windows or counters in the pharmacy, one for male patients and the other for female patients. Depending on the crowd or number of outpatients coming to the hospitals, the authorities may open more counters. At least one, if required, more pharmacists will receive prescriptions through these counters and dispense the medicines.

Outpatients receive their medicines on the prescriptions given to them by the doctors of that particular hospital only (not by other doctors). The medicines are supplied either free of cost (as in government hospitals) or on payment (as in private hospitals). Free medicine cases directly get medicines from the pharmacy. Payment cases, pay the cash at the cash counter of the hospital (or to the dispensing pharmacist himself), produce the receipt along with the prescription to the pharmacy and get the medicines.

Drugs are then dispensed to the patients or their helpers along with necessary instructions regarding their use, storage etc., orally as well as in written form on the containers or envelopes of the medicine. The prescription or the small piece of paper (token) is retained by the pharmacist. He files the retained prescription or 'token' after accounts were written for the drugs mentioned in it, along with the patient's hospital registration number and date. If the case sheets and prescriptions are retained, they are sent back to the hospital patient registration counter, after accounting as above, from where the patients get them on their subsequent visit. This method has been followed till recently in all hospitals, but nowadays, computers are used not only in main drug stores but also in the dispensary of the big hospitals to account for the drugs dispensed. However, it is still in practice in small hospitals.

Usually, seating arrangements are made for the outpatients to sit during the waiting period to get the drugs. Similar dispensing counters are opened in various places of the hospital depending upon the requirement or policy of the hospital. Sometimes special counters are opened to dispense to a special category of patients like Non gazetted Government officers (NGGO).

Dispensing to Inpatients

There are four systems in general use for distributing or dispensing drugs to inpatients. They are,

1. Individual prescription order system.
2. Complete floor stock system.
3. Combination of the above two systems and
4. Unit dose distribution system.

1. **Individual prescription order system**

   This system is generally followed in small and private hospitals where big wards for dozens of patients are not available. As the name implies, patients are given prescriptions individually since there may be a desirability for individualised service. In these small hospitals number of small rooms form the inpatient area, with 2 to 4 beds in each room. Sometimes individual rooms are also provided. Hence, here bulk stock of drugs inwards (as followed in the next type of system) is not feasible. The patients receive the drugs either from the pharmacy of the hospital, if available, or purchase them from an outside pharmacy and keep it ready. The duty nurse administers the drug as per the direction written in the prescription or case sheet. The advantages of this system are

1. Prescription is dispensed by a pharmacist.
2. As drugs are not stored in this inpatient area, there is closer control over the inventory by a pharmacist.
3. Patient can interact with all the members of the health care team, viz, the doctor, nurse and pharmacist.

The main disadvantage is the possible delay in getting the required drugs by the patients and increased cost.

2. Complete floor stock system

In this system, medicines are brought from the main pharmacy and stored in a cupboard in each ward/floor of the hospital complex. The nurse of the ward is in charge for these medicines. They distribute the drugs to the inpatients and account for them. Under this system, the nursing station carries both 'charge' and 'non charge' patient medications. Rarely used expensive medicines are omitted from floor stock but are dispensed upon receipt of a prescription for any individual patients. Selection of drugs to be stored in each floor/ward is done by the PTC of the hospital. In short, this is a mini pharmacy inside the ward – a ward pharmacy – but without a pharmacist. This system is used most often in government and other hospitals in which charges are not collected from the patient or when the 'all-inclusive' rate is used for charging. The followings are the advantages and disadvantages of the system.

Advantages

1. Drugs are readily available in the ward.
2. There is no need to return the drugs to pharmacies or stores.
3. Pharmacy workload is reduced and
4. Consequently, the number of pharmacists required is also reduced.

Disadvantages

1. Pharmacist's services are eliminated (since dispensing is done by nurses).
2. Workload of nurses increases.
3. There are greater chances for the pilferage of drugs as they are stored in dozens of wards.

4. For the same reason, more drugs need to be purchased and consequently cost to the hospital increases.
5. Medication errors may increase, as there is no review of prescriptions by the pharmacists.
6. Proper storage facilities need to be provided in each ward necessitating capital expenses. If not provided, drugs may deteriorate and become dangerous to the patients.

3. Combination of systems 1 and 2

In some hospitals combination of the above two systems is followed. Individual prescription order system is the main means of distributing drugs to the patients and also limited use of floor stock. This combination system is probably the most commonly used system in medium and large hospitals, where there are a number of small rooms for patients, known as special wards and big halls as general wards available.

4. Unit dose distribution system

"Unit dose medications are those medications, which are ordered, packed, handled, administered and charged in multiples of single dose units containing a predetermined amount of drug or supply sufficient for one regular dose, application or use". If drugs are supplied in bulk packing, unit doses were felt necessary for dispensing to the inpatients by the nurses, as otherwise they are required to make calculations, measuring, weighing and packing to administer some drugs to the inpatients in order to avoid such unfamiliar workload to the nurses, a unit dose system was introduced. It should not be confused with what we now call a unit dose. In the above system, medicines are not to be send to the wards in bulk containers, instead, they are subdivided, prepacked for a dose and labelled. Then as per the request of ward nurses, they are sent in a required number of unit doses to the ward.

With the introduction and widespread use of tablets and capsules, these works for the pharmacist are highly minimised. Tablets and capsules are the best ready-to-use, unit dose forms, available in strips or blister packing. Nevertheless, few drugs like powders and cough syrups are still supplied to the hospitals in bulk containers.

The unit dose system under discussion can be best understood by the following example: consider an inpatient is prescribed cough syrup. If only 5 L jars or 500 ml bottle packing of cough syrup is supplied to the hospital, the pharmacist has no option but to send one full container to the ward. Then nurses need to measure the dose every time, and give it to the patient from the bulk container and keep the balance quantity within the ward.

How to account for this supply in stores or dispensary is the problem. The quantity supplied cannot be debited in one patients account, nor can it be unaccounted till all the supply is consumed. Hence there is a compulsion to go for a unit dose system or smaller packing, which requires empty containers, workspace, and equipment for filling, sealing, labelling etc., in the dispensary.

Nowadays, this problem is solved by requesting the drug supplier to the hospital or hospital manufacturing unit to supply both bulk packing (for outpatient dispensing) and unit dose or small packing (for inpatients).

However, as the "distribution of drugs to the inpatients by nurses" is still followed in the majority of hospitals, the unit dose system's advantages and disadvantages have to be studied.

Advantages

1. Workload for nurses reduced.
2. Wastage of drugs is reduced as unused unit doses can be returned to the pharmacy and need not be discarded as in bulk packing.
3. Maintenance of records is made easy as they are maintained in multiplies of unit doses.
4. Accurate delivery of medication (in the form of unit doses) is ensured due to stringent repacking conditions and expert's (pharmacist's) handling.
5. Above all, the unit doses are supplied with proper labels indicating the name of the medicine, its strength, quantity, and expiry date etc., thereby, wrong administration can be minimised.

Disadvantages

1. Cost of medicines goes up due to smaller packing or re-packing.
2. Require more space for storage.
3. Capital expenses need to be made to establish a repacking unit in the hospital if the drugs are not supplied in unit doses.
4. The root cause for the problem is the distribution of drugs to the inpatients by nurses [not by pharmacists].

Other Systems of Dispensing to Inpatients

As discussed above, the main disadvantage of the above systems is dispensing by non-pharmacists. Pharmacists are deprived of their work, and hence their expertise, experience and service cannot be used in dispensing, leading to many problems pointed out as disadvantages of these systems. In order to overcome this problem, some hospitals have introduced a system in which the inpatient prescription or its copy is sent to the main dispensary, where the pharmacist reviews the prescription and dispenses the medicines as follows:

1. **Basket (or) envelopes method**

   In this method, the prescribed drugs for a particular patient are put in a basket or envelope with their methods of use and other details and sent to the ward concerned. There the nurse administers the drug to the particular patient and conveys the directions of the pharmacist written on the envelope or on a paper kept inside the basket. Next day the same basket or envelope is returned to the dispensary for further dispensing of drugs written.

   Thus the main disadvantage of the non-handling of prescriptions by the pharmacist is solved in this method. The pharmacist is able to find out incompatibility or drug interaction possibilities and other connected problems by handling the prescription. Thus he is able to help the doctor in selecting a suitable drug/formulation for the particular patient. However, still, there is one deficiency in this method, the pharmacist-patient direct dialogue is not there, and whatever the pharmacist wants to tell the patient is conveyed through a third party- the nurses.

   Thus the basket or envelop system does not solve all the problems of inpatient dispensing.

2. **Mobile dispensing system**

   It utilises a specially constructed stainless steel truck where essential and frequently used medicines are taken to the wards. A worker of the pharmacy department pushes this truck to the ward accompanied by a pharmacist. It is stopped in front of each ward or in specified places, and the pharmacist does dispensing to the inpatients by collecting their prescriptions individually from them. The process is similar to the distribution of food and diet to the in patients by hospital authorities three times a day, supervised by the dieticians of the hospital. The frequency of delivery of medicines and the hours during which the mobile unit will visit the ward will be selected in cooperation with the nursing service.

   The main advantages of this system are pharmacist himself does dispensing, and hence, his services are available for consultation by patients, nurses and medical staff. However, the disadvantage of this method is the non-availability of all medicines in the truck as well as space for keeping the required quantity. Thus, the pharmacist or his assistant is compelled more often to return to the dispensary to bring and supply non-available items to the inpatients. Though two main problems of previous methods, prescription handling and conveying instructions directly to the inpatients, are solved, a new problem of inadequate availability of drugs arises in this method.

3. Satellite pharmacy

These are nothing but branches of the main hospital pharmacy functioning around the hospital in a different block if the hospital is spread over a vast area in several buildings or on a few other floors if it is a multi-storied building.

The main pharmacy will supply the medicines to these satellite or mini pharmacies. Patients and/or nurses in charge of the ward obtain their requirements of drugs from these satellite pharmacies instead of going to the main pharmacy. Sometimes these satellite pharmacies are established to cater to a special or specified category of peoples like government officers, legislatures, patients from special clinics etc. Thus it distributes drugs to both inpatients and unique outpatients. However, these pharmacies will have less stock only compared to the main pharmacy, which receives its supply in bulk from hospital stores.

Advantage of satellite pharmacy service is that the patients are able to get the medicine quickly without spending much time. Moreover, the large crowd gathering before the main pharmacy and consequent problems are avoided.

The disadvantage is an increase in inventory and subsequent cost. Nevertheless, almost all the problems in dispensing to inpatients are more or less solved in this method. Hence, modern hospitals or renovated old hospitals are equipped with satellite pharmacies (e.g.) Rajiv Gandhi Government General Hospital, Chennai.

Dispensing of Narcotics or Controlled Substances

During the course of dispensing to the patients, the pharmacist has to dispense narcotic drugs also. Narcotics are drugs that produce deleterious effects such as undue depression or stimulation of the human brain resulting in effects like euphoria, personality destabilizing effects, addiction etc. Hence there are certain conditions and procedures to dispense such drugs enforced by the government through the drugs control department. These procedures must be known to all dispensing pharmacists, and they are expected to follow those guidelines in letter and spirit. Failing which, may result in prosecution by the drug inspectors and/or police personnel.

Let us first look at the general conditions for dispensing narcotics, followed by specific procedures to be followed by pharmacists while dispensing to outpatients and inpatients of a hospital.

General Conditions

1. No narcotic drug should be dispensed without a written prescription from a registered medical practitioner.
2. Narcotic drugs should not be dispensed for more than one day use unless specifically prescribed by the physician.
3. Narcotic prescriptions should be retained in the pharmacy after dispensing the drug or returned to the patient after putting the rubber stamp 'issued/dispensed' and signature (with date) of the pharmacist on the prescription. If retained, the prescriptions must be kept in a separate file for inspection by drug inspectors.
4. No prescription for narcotics may be refilled. If the procedure mentioned in 3 above is properly followed, no prescription will be coming to the pharmacy for refilling.
5. No controlled substance (narcotic), which is a drug, may be dispensed other than for a medical purpose.
6. Prescription for narcotics must be written in ink and shall not bear any erasing or alteration. It must be signed by the doctor, along with his name and registration number rubber stamp.
7. Prescriptions for narcotics must be complete in all aspects, that is, it must contain the full address and diagnosis of the patient, as well as the doctor's hospital address and phone number.

Hospital Procedure for Dispensing Narcotics

1. Responsibility for narcotics in the hospital

In general, the administrative head of the hospital is responsible for the proper safeguarding and handling of narcotics within the hospital. Chief pharmacist is responsible for the purchase, storage and maintenance of account and proper dispensing of narcotics in particular. Similarly, the head nurse of a ward is responsible for the proper storage and use of controlled substances (narcotics) in the ward.

2. Dispensing to inpatients

As the administration of narcotic drugs to the inpatients is by the nurses, and these drugs are not given directly to the patient for self-administration, there is always greater control over its use compared to outpatients.

Hence, the procedure is simple in that a separate copy of the prescription should be written for narcotics for inpatients, along with the usual prescription written on the case sheet by the treating physician. This separate prescription must be complete in all aspects as described above and sent to the dispensary. The drugs supplied are kept under lock and key by the ward nurse and administered to the patient as per the directions written on the case sheet.

A *pro re nata* (*prn*) (occasionally) or *si opus sit* (*SOS*) (whenever necessary) prescriptions for narcotics must be discouraged except under special circumstances. The doctor may give orders by telephone in case of necessity. Then the nurse writes the order on the doctor's prescription sheet, stating that it is a telephone order. The nurse has to write the doctor's name and put her own initials. The doctor must then sign the order within 24 hours. Similarly, a doctor may give verbal orders for narcotic drugs in an extreme emergency where time does not permit writing the order. The nurse must write the order on the prescription sheet, and the doctor should sign it within 24 hours.

The doctor should not write prescriptions for narcotics for his own use. Narcotics obtained for ward use should not be issued for home use by the patients on discharge. These are all the procedures followed in the majority of the hospitals but may have additional or reduced conditions in a few hospitals.

3. Dispensing to outpatients

The prescription for narcotics to outpatients must contain the following information:

(a) Patient's full name
(b) Patient's address
(c) Hospital number
(d) Date
(e) Name and strength of the drug
(f) Quantity to be dispensed
(g) Directions for use
(h) Signature of the physician

The prescription must be written in ink and must not bear any correction. Narcotics should not be dispensed for more than one day's use unless prescribed specifically by the physician. Automatic stop order for narcotics after one day's use is enforced by many hospitals in this regard. All other general conditions for dispensing narcotics are applicable to the dispensing of narcotics to outpatients.

Distribution of Drugs to ICCU/ICU/NICU/ Emergency Wards

Distribution of drugs for intensive care or critical cases is one of the important duties of pharmacists, hence he should be thorough and ready for that assignment. As the drugs are administered in an emergency or critical situation, they should be ready for administration to patients and must bear adequate labels for identification, strength or potency, route of administration and special instructions, if any, apart from usual information like Batch No, Expiry date etc.

The following are the drugs usually required for critical or emergency cases: 1. Cardiovascular drugs 2. Antibiotics 3. Analgesics and Muscle relaxants 4. Respiratory drugs 5. Fluid and Electrolytes 6. Anticoagulation 7. Renal drugs 8. Endocrine drugs 9. G.I Drugs and 10. Hypnotics and Sedatives.

These drugs are kept ready in the hospital's drug store and distributed to the following units as and when required.

1. Intensive Care Units [ICU]: It is one of the very important unit of the hospital where patients, after severe injury or illness, is admitted and taken care of with life support systems and medicines. All the medicines listed above are stocked in this unit in sufficient quantities and replenished by the pharmacist every day. Thus the constant quantity of drugs is available in ICU as in emergency wards. That apart depends on the patient's condition, other medicines may be requested, and the pharmacist must be able to supply it without delay.
2. Intensive Critical Care units [ICCU]: This is also called an Intensive Coronary Care Unit or Intensive Cardiac Care Unit. But, the name Intensive Critical Care Unit seems to be more suitable as not only cardiac patients even other patients may require critical care on admission or subsequently. Hence restricting an important ward to only one group of patients may not be ideal. However, in practice, there is no clear-cut difference between the two. These are all dependent on the hospital, its facilities and its policies. Some people declare that both ICC and ICCU are one and the same. Anyhow, as the name implies, the patients admitted to this unit require critical, round-the-clock, intensive treatment, hence all the medicines listed above are supplied to this unit. Sometimes pharmacists need to procure some drugs very urgently and supply them to this unit. Hence he should be ready with all the information about the supplier including his phone number, method of delivery, the time required for delivery etc.
3. Neonatal Intensive Care Unit [NICU]. Here newborn babies are taken care of intensively if required. Usually, premature babies are maintained here with the help of incubators. All pediatric formulations required for intensive-care neonatal babies should be supplied and stocked in this unit. Pharmacists must ensure the availability of those pediatric formulations.
4. Emergency wards: As indicated above, in this ward, all emergency drugs are supplied. They are stored in a special cabinet in the ward.

They are selected and limited quantities of drugs packaged in single-unit containers. That apart, I.V. solutions, irrigating solutions, eye-tray medications, medicines for cardio-pulmonary resuscitation and refrigerated drugs are stored in areas of ready access. A list of emergency drugs is given in the previous chapter.

Automated Drug Dispensing Systems and Devices

One of the recent methods of drug distribution is an automated drug dispensing system where computer-programmed devices are used. But for using these systems, there are a few preconditions a pharmacist must fulfil. William E. Hasson lists them as follows:

(a) When utilising automated [mechanical and/or electronic] devices, it is mandatory that provision be made to provide suitable pharmaceutical services in the event of failure of the device.

(b) Such mechanical or electronic drug storage and dispensing devices may require repacking of drug dosage forms from the manufacturer's original container. These repacking must assure the stability of each drug and meet pharmacopoeial standards for the packaging and storing of drugs, in addition to meeting all other standards of good pharmacy practice.

(c) The automated devices should permit accuracy in accounting as well as dispensing.

Why Automated Drug Dispensing?

Manual medicine dispensing is rife with challenges. It is tedious, repetitive and error-prone. Hence nowadays, drug dispensing is automated in big hospitals in developed countries, and the concept is slowly picking up in countries where there is a shortage of pharmacists. As pharmacy automation is the electronic process of distributing, sorting, packaging and counting prescription medicines, it is widely used in those countries. The main purpose of using it, as per their claim, is improving efficiency, minimising labour costs and improving accuracy.

Modern automation process is used to 1. Dispensing medicines 2. Syncing records, and 3. Complying with regulations.

Advantages

It helps the pharmacist in the following A] Accuracy and Speed, B] Space savings, C] Narcotics security, D] Inventory Management. Apart from the above advantages, the automated dispensing system has the following benefits for the institution and healthcare team

1. Having medication storage at the point of care

2. Prevents communication or prescribing errors
3. Quick and easy removal and return of drugs from the dispensing cabinet. Since automated dispensing cabinets [ADC] are not located in pharmacies, they are considered a decentralised medication distribution system. They can be installed in ICUs, Wards etc. These ADCs are interfaced with the central pharmacy computer.

Disadvantages

1. They reduce the Job opportunity of Pharmacists. It is a serious question how much it is suitable for a big country like India with huge unemployment of pharmacists.
2. Illiteracy, Power failure and similar problems should be considered before going for ADCs.
3. Replacing men with machines may not be a good idea for technical and life and death matters.

Questions

Short Answer Questions

1. Who is an ambulatory patient?
2. Write a note on the mobile pharmacy.
3. Write briefly about satellite pharmacy.
4. Write short notes on the unit dose system.

Long Answer Questions

5. Write an essay about dispensing to inpatients.
6. Detail the procedure to be followed for dispensing narcotics.
7. Describe the complete floor stock system and its advantages and disadvantages.
8. Write in detail about dispensing drugs to ICU, ICCU, NICU etc.
9. Write a note on Automated Drug Dispensing Systems and devices.

   Discuss its advantages and disadvantages.

CHAPTER 7

COMPOUNDING IN HOSPITALS

Pharmacy practice in modern times has changed enormously, that compounding in its original sense is not in practice in almost all hospitals. Nevertheless, it is still being practised in its wider meaning and application. It remains an important practice to meet unique or specific needs, providing specialised formulations for individual patients in circumstances where commercially available medicines may not be appropriate. Examples are dosing for pediatric, geriatric or other vulnerable populations.

Thus compounding earlier done, before the pharma industry supplied all medicines required in hospitals, was for all patients to prepare mainly mixtures, emulsions, and external use preparations, have now changed. Now compounding combines or alters ingredients to create a medication tailored to the unique medical needs of an individual patient. It is now carried out in the treatment of rare diseases, in clinical trials, in a situation where the strength or dosage of medicine needs to be customised, in reformulating a drug to exclude unwanted non-essential ingredients and for changing the form of medication for patients who have difficulty swallowing.

The Food and Drug Administration of America defines compounding as a practice in which a licenced pharmacist or licenced physician mixes or alters ingredients of a drug to create a medication tailored to the needs of an individual patient. The USP defines compounding as the preparation, mixing, assembling, altering, packaging and labelling of a drug, drug-delivery device or device in accordance with a licenced practitioner's prescription. Thus the preparation of total parenteral nutrition [TPN] and intravenous admixture [IVA] in hospitals which are explained below, are coming under compounding.

Bulk Compounding

As the name implies, it is nothing but the preparation of formulations in hospitals, in bulk, to meet the needs of many patients. Before India's independence and up to the 1970s, our hospitals were preparing mixtures, ointments and lotions in bulk to dispense to the patients coming to the hospitals in large numbers. They were called stock mixtures in those days. They are actually bulk compounding only, but to reduce the storage containers and space required to store them, they were prepared in concentrated forms and diluted 1:4 or 1:5 or even 1:10 with distilled or demineralised water and then dispensed. For the preparation of distilled water, Manesty Still was installed in Dispensaries. Similarly, ointments were also prepared in bulk, up to a kilogram and more, and then dispensed in prescribed quantities like 10 or 15 grams to patients in butter papers, wide-mouth bottles, or collapsible tubes, if available. Thus bulk compounding was in practice in our hospitals.

Those medicines were cheaper, readily available and, more importantly, had good pharmacological effects. Both patients and doctors were satisfied and happy with those preparations. Hence all the patients coming to the hospital used to bring an empty bottle in those days in anticipation of taking the liquid medicine dispensed. Even if it is not prescribed, they used to demand with the pharmacist [compounders, then!] 'Gas medicine' [carminative mixture] or 'Cough medicine' or 'Diarrhoea medicine'. Pharmacists sometimes oblige, so they have huge respect and are popular with patients! Those were the golden days for pharmacy! As compounding is a technical work carried out by pharmacists, they were treated with regard and respect by society and colleagues. Now pharmacists lost those technical works to the pharma industry and were reduced to mere drug-distributing machines; hence, non-pharmacists started occupying hospital and community pharmacies!

To regain the lost glory, pharmacists cannot return to compounding but should try to deliver value-added services like counselling, guiding, maintaining patient medication profile, monitoring drug therapy, B.P and /or Sugar testing, etc., in their pharmacy.

Total Parenteral Nutrition and Intravenous Admixture

Introduction

Total Parenteral Nutrition and Intravenous admixture are essentially part of manufacturing or compounding activities, and hence it is more appropriate to study them next to compounding in hospitals. Needless to point out, the above-mentioned works can be carried out better by manufacturing pharmacists in a formulation manufacturing unit than in any other set-up, including a dispensary of the hospitals, as all the space and facilities for compounding, mixing, filtering, filling, and testing are readily available in the hospital manufacturing units. Without such manufacturing facilities in the hospital, medical practitioners in the hospitals are finding it difficult to get the appropriate formulations to suit the specific needs of particular patients. They are either compelled to use available formulations or administer multiple formulations to the patient, making the treatment process much more complicated. Hence they welcome these facilities and expertise in their hospitals.

Total Parenteral Nutrition

Definition

Intravenous administration of calories, nitrogen and other nutrients in sufficient quantities to achieve tissue synthesis and anabolism is called Total Parenteral Nutrition (TPN). Long ago, this was described as hyperalimentation, but nowadays, it is referred to as TPN, as this name is more suitable and explains the technique.

Indications

From the above definition, it is clear that parenteral nutrition (PN) is the intravenous administration of a nutritionally balanced and physically and chemically stable, sterile solution. It is indicated if the gastrointestinal tract is inaccessible, inadequate or inappropriate to meet the patient's ongoing nutritional needs. Parenteral nutrition may meet the total nutritional requirements of the patient or supplement the enteral feed or diet.

It is given to patients who are unable to eat due to carcinoma or extensive burns or who refuse to eat, like geriatric cases. It is also indicated to young patients suffering from anorexia nervosa and surgical patients who should not be given food orally.

After the patient's condition is improved, depending on his external food intake, the TPN should be gradually reduced and should not be stopped abruptly.

Composition of TPN

The objective of including various components of TPN is to provide appropriate sources and amounts of all the building blocks in a single daily admixture. Thus, in addition to water, six main groups of nutrients must be included in the TPN formulation. They are amino acids, glucose, a lipid with essential fatty acids, Vitamins, Trace elements and Electrolytes.

Water: In general, an adult patient requires fluids up to 20 to 40 ml/kg/day. This is regulated by homeostasis of the body in normal people and may be ineffective in patients. Hence the appropriate amount of water should be administered to the patient to avoid over or under-hydration. Some of the factors affecting fluid requirements are dehydration or overload, fever, acute anabolic state, high environmental temperature, or low or high humidity, abnormal GI loss, burns or open wounds, blood loss or transfusion, drug therapy and cardiac or renal failure. Taking into consideration all these factors, the fluid input is either increased or reduced.

Amino acids: 20 amino acids are required for protein synthesis and metabolism. A majority of these can be synthesised by our body. There are some eight amino acids which are called essential amino acids because they cannot be synthesised, whereas even some of the synthesised amino acids may not be sufficient in diseased conditions. Neonates, infants and children may need some amino acids due to ineffective or immature metabolic pathways. All these factors are taken into consideration while formulating TPN. Crystalline amino acids serve as a source of nitrogen in TPN fluids. The crystalline amino acids injections contain all the essential and non-essential amino acids in the L form. For optimum use of amino acids and for promoting tissue regeneration, the nitrogen to calorie ratio should be 1:150. Amino acid solutions are hypertonic and should not be administered alone into the peripheral circulation.

Glucose: Glucose is the ideal source of carbohydrates. Glucose, a 5% solution, is isotonic with blood, but to meet the energy requirement of 2500 calories/day, this concentration may not be sufficient as it provides only 170 calories/litre. Hence higher concentrations, say 25%, is administered, but it causes phlebitis if administered directly to peripheral veins and hence should be given by a central vein (sub-clavian vein into the super vena cava) or after diluting with compatible solutions like amino acid injections to reduce the toxicity.

Lipid: Lipid emulsions are used as a source of energy and for providing essential fatty acids, like linoleic acid and linolenic acid. They are energy rich and directly administered into peripheral veins as they are isotonic with blood. Earlier, soyabean oil was used in TPN formulations; nowadays, olive oil, fish oil and medium-chain triglycerides are used. Lipid clearance should be monitored by the clinical pharmacist for diabetic and other patients with impaired renal or hepatic functions.

Vitamins: The daily requirement of both water-soluble and fat-soluble vitamins should be added to the TPN formulation. It is usually added in the form of multivitamin infusion concentrate. Combinations of different vitamin formulations are used, as no formulation meets the guideline requirement of all vitamins.

Electrolytes: The requirement of electrolytes used varies with the individual patient, and the electrolyte content in the amino acid injections also should be taken into account while deciding the TPN components. The following is the concentration range of electrolytes to be used.

Sodium	-	100-120 mEq.
Potassium	-	80-120 mEq.
Magnesium	-	8-16 mEq.
Calcium	-	5-10 mEq.
Chloride	-	100-120 mEq. and
Phosphate	-	40-60 mEq.

Trace elements: There are ten trace elements required for the body. They are iron, copper, zinc, fluorine, manganese, iodine, cobalt, selenium, molybdenum and chromium, out of this, iron can be administered separately from the PN fluids. Others are a concern only in long-term cases and can be added when required. Some of the factors to be considered while deciding the requirement of micronutrients (including vitamins) are baseline nutritional state, increased loss, increased requirement and organ function like liver or kidney impairments.

Advantages of TPN and its Handling

Parenteral nutrition was administered from a series of separate bottles earlier. Healthcare staff had to accurately and safely manage different trip sets, infusion rates and infusion times. Now it is possible to administer the total requirement of a patient's nutrition from a single daily bag of a pharmaceutically stable formulation.

There are many advantages of TPN. They are: It is convenient and time-saving, permit optimum utilisation, reduces the infection risk, reduces the risk of error, reduces the scope for incompatibility, and makes easy storage and stock management and the possibility of home management. There are a few disadvantages like potential time delay in preparing specific TPN, potential wastage of TPN if patients need changes, also a variation of physical and chemical stability need to be known for storage and infusion time.

Overload of fluid, nutrition and electrolytes can have serious consequences; hence an infusion control pump must be used along with a compatible infusion set. TPN should be administered when it is at room temperature, hence it should be removed from the refrigerator 3 hours before administering. Initially, it should be given at a slow rate for the first 24 hours, later, it can be increased if the patient tolerates it. The patient should be monitored for adverse events like nausea, vomiting, sweating and flushing.

Formulation Problems

After identifying the various nutrients and their quantities required by a patient, it is necessary to formulate a physically and chemically stable sterile preparation.

These preparations, at times, contain more than 50 ingredients and hence are extremely complex. Reference books should be consulted before making a preparation. The following are the problems of a TPN formulation.

1. **Physical stability:** Precipitation and lipid destabilisation are the two important problems of the physical stability of TPN. Precipitation may occur due to various factors like pH, temperature, presence of amino acids, magnesium, calcium and phosphorus and mixing order. Lipid destabilisation results in creaming flocculation and coalescence.
2. **Chemical stability:** It is identified by the chemical degradation of the vitamins, and amino acids, oxidation of vitamin C, photolysis of vitamin A, and photo-oxidation of vitamin E are common. They can be avoided by protecting the preparation from light and high temperatures.
3. **Microbial stability:** TPN formulation itself is a highly nutritious medium for microbial growth. Hence it should be sterilised properly and handled carefully so as not to contaminate the product. As with any IV infusion, TPN also must be carefully examined visually and then used.
4. **Drug stability:** PN should not be mixed with other drugs as far as possible, as it will affect the above stabilities of the PN as well the drug being mixed. It may also affect the bioavailability of the drug. A strict aseptic technique should be adopted to minimise the risk of contaminating the line while adding a drug.

In addition to the above problems, particulate matter contamination during administration and photo-degradation during storage and transport must be taken care of by using the terminal in-line filters, quality trip sets and raw materials, and protection from light.

I.V. [Intravenous] Admixtures

Introduction

The mixing of intravenous solutions with additional substances is done by Nurses and House surgeons or Doctors in India, even today in the majority of the hospitals. It is done on the assumption that all the Injections or sterile preparations are the same and can be mixed with IV fluids. Just because all they add to IV fluids are also sterile, they believe nothing will happen to those fluids. Obviously, they look only at the sterility aspect of IV fluid and added drugs and have no knowledge whatsoever about its stability, solubility, pH, incompatibility etc. Now, at least a section of this healthcare team has realised that the IV Admixture is a sort of Injection manufacturing process and requires the skills of a manufacturing pharmacist. Still, a vast majority of these peoples are unaware and has to be educated by pharmacists and in the meanwhile, to avoid mixing of additional drugs, various devices are developed by IV trip set manufacturers with different ports (openings) for additives in the set itself (VENTPLAN) or at the point of insertion of a needle into the body of the patient, thus making the admixture of drugs an occasional requirement. However, a pharmacist must know the task of preparing IV admixture.

Definition

When one or more sterile products are added to an IV fluid for administration, the resulting mixture is known as IV admixture.

Objectives of Preparation of IV Admixtures

1. IV admixture must be done under strict aseptic conditions.
2. Drug interactions should be avoided by the correct choice of additives and mixing techniques.
3. The final product should be appropriately labelled, dispensed and stored.

Suitability of Pharmacists

As adding any ingredient to a formulation is a manufacturing activity, only a technical hand with the knowledge of the process is suitable. Thus a pharmacist who undergoes training and education in the manufacturing process and learn about the physical, chemical and pharmacological properties of drugs during his graduation is the perfect suit for the process than anybody else.

Moreover, to maintain the characteristics of sterile products, namely, sterility and freedom from particulate matter and pyrogen, it is imperative that they be performed by pharmacists in a suitable environment using aseptic techniques.

Purpose and uses of IV Admixture Service by Pharmacists

If the IV admixture service is undertaken by the pharmacist,

(a) It saves the nursing time,

(b) It provides for screening of physical and chemical incompatibilities by him

(c) It minimises calculation errors and medication errors

(d) It centralises the responsibility on the pharmacist rather than on multiple workers of the health care team

(e) Specific directions on the label, like rate of infusion, are possible and

(f) It provides for solutions not commercially available.

Thus IV admixture service by pharmacists has many advantages and uses.

Preparation Area

Laminar flow Hoods provide an area for aseptic handling of IV admixture. In laminar flow hoods, the air is filtered through High-Efficiency Particulate Air (HEPA) filter. HEPA filters remove 99.9% of all particles larger than 0.3 μm.

Since microbes are found on particles, the removal of particles results in a flow of air free from both particles and microorganisms. Regardless of the type of laminar airflow, the Hood must be maintained properly to achieve an environment suitable for IV Admixture.

It must be placed in an air-conditioned room, free from any movement in front of it, and its inside workbench should be wiped with a suitable disinfectant 30 minutes before the process. It must be remembered that a laminar flow hood is not a means of sterilisation but only maintain an area for IV admixture if prepared, maintained and used properly by operator with proper aseptic techniques.

Operation and maintenance of Laminar flow Hoods can be had from the supplier and/or manufacturer of it, which should be strictly followed to get the best results.

Mixing of Additional Drugs

These drugs may be injections in ampoules or vials. If solids, they must be reconstituted with suitable diluents before adding them to IV fluid. A new, sterile, disposable syringe should be used for each drug, and its needle may be replaced with a sterile aspirating needle. Aspirating needles have stainless steel or nylon filter with 5 μm pores. Additional drugs are drawn from their containers using this needle and then replaced with the original regular needle.

Some of the additional drugs may be light sensitive, and hence the syringe can be wrapped with aluminium foil and added to the IV fluid. The procedure for adding a drug in an IV fluid will vary depending on the type of IV fluid container.

Usually, an IV admixture is considered as a unit dose. However, if intermittent administration of drugs is essential, three methods are available:

1. Direct IV injection

2. Addition of drug to a pre-determined volume of IV fluid in a volume control chamber attached below the main IV bag or bottle.
3. Use of a second container (mini bottle/bag) with already hanging IV fluid and join them by using the 'Y' tube at the bottom.

Parenteral Incompatibility

When one or more drugs are added to an IV fluid, they may modify the characters of the substances present, resulting in parenteral incompatibility. They are classified into Physical Incompatibility, Chemical Incompatibility and Therapeutic Incompatibility.

Among these, physical incompatibility can be predicted if the chemical properties of added drugs and IV fluids are known. For example, sodium salts of weak acids, such a Phenytoin sodium or Phenobarbital sodium, precipitate as free acids when added to IV fluids with acidic ph. Similarly, calcium salts precipitate when added to an alkaline medium, and water-insoluble substances, such as diazepam, precipitate when added to IV fluids.

Chemical incompatibilities are occurring due to hydrolysis, oxidation, reduction or complexation and can only be detected by analytical methods. An important factor which affects IV admixture is the change in acid-base environment or pH of it. As the solubility and, more importantly, stability of IV fluids depend on a particular pH, they should not be disturbed by added drugs. Though the change in solubility is visible by the precipitation etc., stability changes cannot be viewed. An example of this is the antibiotic penicillin, which is active at pH 6.5 for 24 hours, whereas it is destroyed at pH 3.5 within a short time.

Therapeutic incompatibility is better illustrated in the example of the antagonising effect of penicillin or cortisone on heparin. Thus, though it is impossible to predict and prevent all parenteral incompatibilities, their occurrence can be minimised if the pharmacist concerned with IV admixture consults all the available literatures from parenteral manufacturers.

Quality Control

In order to maintain standards and quality of IV admixture, each hospital should have written procedures for each and every step of preparing IV admixture. Starting from the selection of additives to the final administration and monitoring of the patient, it is essential to maintain high standards. Suitable training programmes and re-orientation programmes should be arranged for the staff concerned with IV admixture.

In fact, all these operations are to be considered equivalent, in no way inferior, to the current Good Manufacturing Practices followed by manufacturing industries and insisted by Government through the Drugs Control Department.

Questions

Short Answer Questions

1. What is total parenteral nutrition?
2. Define IV Admixture.
3. What are the purpose and uses of IV admixture service by pharmacists?
4. What is compounding in hospitals?
5. What is bulk compounding?

Long Answer Questions

6. Describe the composition of total parenteral nutrition. What are the problems encountered during its preparation?
7. How IV admixtures are prepared? Add a note on parenteral incompatibility.
8. Why a TPN is prepared? Describe its handling and advantage.
9. Write in detail about compounding in hospitals

CHAPTER 8

RADIO PHARMACEUTICALS

A Radiopharmaceutical is a preparation used for diagnosis and therapy, used *in vivo*, containing a radionuclide in the form of an element, a simple salt or a complex and may exist in the form of a solid, liquid or gas.

Purchase

Unlike general drugs, radiopharmaceuticals cannot be procured from wholesalers or stockists. It is under the control of the Government of India, and hence it has to be purchased from Government agencies only.

Moreover, the supply cannot take a long time, as in the case of general drugs, as the radioisotopes are subject to decay and have a half-life. It should reach the potential user before it loses its activity considerably; hence, usually, it is supplied by overnight delivery through airways.

While ordering it, shipping or delivery schedule, ratio activity decay etc., are to be taken into account.

Storage

Radiopharmaceuticals should be stored as per the rules. They should be in the nuclear medicine hot lab, which is a limited-access area. Hot lab is a separate room for handling nuclear materials above the tracer level. It should have a strengthened fume cub- board with an airflow away from the operator. Additional safety measures, like a separate entrance for the room, are provided to avoid the transport of supplies through this room. For storing radiopharmaceuticals, a separate steel cub board with lock and key and lead containers are provided. It is to protect the handler as the radio-pharmaceuticals are potentially radioactive.

Dispensing or Handling of Radiopharmaceuticals

Though radiopharmaceuticals are prescribed for patients, they are not directly dispensed to them. Instead, they are handed over to the trained healthcare professionals of the hospital and then administered to the patient by the authorised doctor. Therefore, radiopharmaceuticals are dispensed in unit doses. While deciding the dose and other related matters, patient factors such as age, weight, the surface area of the body and γ camera sensitivity etc., must be considered both by the doctor and the pharmacist. Needless to mention, the decay corrections, to accommodate from when the radiopharmaceutical was prepared to the time it is actually administered to the patient, should be made for each radiopharmaceutical.

If injections of radiopharmaceuticals are to be given, they are administered with lead-lined special syringes supplied with the product. All the above operations should be made by using appropriate information on all products and accessories and at the place provided for them.

For example, labs for radiopharmaceuticals must be provided with unidirectional flow work stations-the fuming cub-board. Drainage should be provided as per standards dictated by a government agency.

After receiving the necessary information and instructions from the licenced physician who is authorised to use Radiopharmaceuticals, the pharmacist may require to make necessary calculations to arrive at the dose to be dispensed. It may be verified by the physician concerned. Then pharmacist transfers the required dose from the stock container using a remote-controlled pipette in a special laminar flow table provided for it. He has to put it in a paper cup within a lead container and transport it safely to the patient care area (Special ward) for administration to the patient.

Radioactive isotopes are administered to patients for the treatment of various conditions, e.g. radioactive iodine for hyperthyroidism, radioactive gold for malignant diffusions, and radioactive phosphorus for malignant haematological conditions. They emit β and γ rays, and exposure should be reduced to the minimum by,

1. Avoiding contamination of clothing and skin from body secretions of the patient
2. Keeping the time close to the patient, as short as possible and
3. Keeping as great a distance from the patient as possible when in the unit.

Disposal

When the radiopharmaceuticals are no longer usable, they are either returned to the nuclear pharmacy service provider or supplier for disposal. Alternatively, they are separated according to their half-life in the hot lab until its radiation decays to that of the level prevailing in the area. Then it can be disposed of as per the biomedical waste disposal procedure.

The following precautions and procedures should be followed while disposing of radiopharmaceutical waste and contaminations by it.

1. Wastes should not be allowed to accumulate. They should be disposed of as early as possible. Otherwise, accumulated waste may increase the background radiation, and it is a danger to the hospital workers and the general public.
2. As for as possible, avoid mixing different radiopharmaceutical wastes. If unavoidable, mix radiopharmaceuticals of the same half-life. Mixing longer half-life material with shorter half-life material will delay the disposal of the latter.
3. Waste is not disposed of or poured down the sink or put along with other waste, or incinerated.
4. Usually, the radiation safety officer of the hospital will dispose of the waste by following the procedure prescribed by Atomic Energy Commission. He may follow any one or more of the following suitable techniques like precipitation, evaporation, adsorption, incineration, dilution or addition of stable isotope to reduce specific activity to a point at which quick disposal is permitted.
5. Air pollution is negligible when a few curies of radiopharmaceuticals are handled. Usually, air from the fuming cub-board is vented very high above the building roof.
6. If lab animals used for experiments are to be disposed of, they are covered with bleaching powder and vermiculate. They are sealed in plastic bags and kept cool until disposed of.
7. Disposing of contamination or Decontamination procedure:
   (a) Spillage should be marked and decontaminated immediately
   (b) Liquid spillage is absorbed by paper tissues or vermiculite.
   (c) Contaminated area washed or cleaned with water or detergent with EDTA or Citric Acid or other complexing agents.
   (d) Powder contaminant is disposed of by fixing it with strippable coating material.
   (e) Glassware should be cleaned quickly with water, detergent and/or complexing agents. Their cleanliness is verified by radioactive tests, which should not be more than one micro curie.

Needless to mention, all the radiopharmaceuticals and their wastes should be properly labelled to ensure safety with the following information, apart from the usual.

1. Name 2. Strength 3. Warning: Material is Radioactive 4. Content of bactericide, and 5. Special mark or number to trace the material's history.

Responsibility of Pharmacists and others in using Radio Isotopes

For their own safety, as well as, the safety of others, pharmacist and others whoever handling or using radio isotopes has the following responsibilities:

1. To receive instruction in radiation safety as determined appropriate by the radiation safety officer.
2. To keep exposure to radiation at the lowest level possible and specifically below the maximum permissible exposure.
3. To wear recommended radiation dosimeters for personnel, such as film badges, pocket ionization chambers and finger dosimeters.
4. To examine his hand, shoes, body and clothing for radio activity and removal of all loose contamination before leaving the laboratory.
5. To use all appropriate protective measures, such as protective clothing, respiratory protection, remote pipetting devices, ventilated and shielded glove box and hoods.
6. To prohibit smoking and eating in radio isotope laboratories.
7. To check working area daily or after each radio isotope procedure.
8. To maintain good lab practices, such as keeping working area and equipment clean and orderly.
9. To use proper labels on equipment being used with radioactive materials.
10. To place all active waste in proper containers, equipped with proper labels.
11. To report immediately the details of a 'spill' or other accident involving radioactive substances to the radiation safety officer.
12. To conduct decontamination procedures as directed by the radiation safety officer.

The above guidelines are given in radio isotope manual prepared by Peter Bent Brigham hospital, Boston. Similar manuals and booklets are issued by others also, who are involved in handling radio pharmaceuticals. Radio isotope committee of each hospital prepares and circulates such instructions to their staff concerned.

Questions

Short Answer Questions

1. What is the need for Radiopharmaceuticals?
2. Write short notes on the storage of radiopharmaceuticals.

Long Answer Questions

3. Write in detail about the disposal of Radiopharmaceuticals
4. Explain the role of the pharmacist in dispensing Radiopharmaceuticals
5. Detail the responsibilities of Pharmacists in Radiopharmaceuticals

CHAPTER 9

APPLICATION OF COMPUTERS IN HOSPITAL PHARMACY PRACTICE

The advent of computers and information technology in the last few decades has revolutionised the entire world; the pharmacy field is not an exemption. Computers have made it easy for many works relating to data collection, storage, retrieval, accounting and manufacturing to go even beyond the world of space science. Hospital pharmacy departments of almost all hospitals started using it, first for purchase, storage and distribution of drugs in the hospital drugs store and dispensing to maintain patient's profile, drug monitoring, analysis and treatment modification in wards. A budding pharmacist must be familiar with its usage and maintenance to be a successful practising pharmacist.

Computers are used in the following area in a hospital pharmacy.

1. Medication order entry
2. Purchasing and Inventory control
3. Preparation of drug labels
4. Drug usage and cost reports
5. Billing
6. Patient profile
7. Drug therapy monitoring
8. Drug therapy problems and management
9. DUR/DUE Reports
10. Maintenance of Hospital Formulary
11. Drug information Centre and
12. I.V admixture and T.P.N detail.

1. **Medication Order Entry**

   In modern hospitals, nowadays, medication orders or prescriptions are issued through computers by doctors, and a copy is sent to dispensaries via computers. A printout of the same is given to the patient. After verification, medicines are dispensed to the patient and entries are made in the relevant records by the pharmacist. By this arrangement, many problem faced by pharmacists and doctors like, misspelling, misreading, illegible handwriting, patients missing prescriptions, mix up at the patient or pharmacist end, wrong entries in records, a lot of time required for manual entries by a pharmacist and many other problems are solved.

2. **Purchase and inventory control:**

   These works are explained elsewhere in another chapter. However, the use of computers in the purchase of drugs and their storage cannot be over-emphasized. The benefits are apparent, not only in drug stores of hospitals but wherever materials are purchased and or stored, computers play a major role. E. tender, E. procurement, e. pharmacy etc., are now in practice everywhere.

3. **Preparation of Drug Labels**

   During the course of dispensing or compounding, a pharmacist needs to label the containers through which they are supplied. Preparation of labels for those containers are made easy by storing standard templates in required numbers in the computer. Required labels of different sizes or shapes, with all the relevant information, are printed using computers and fixed on the drug container. The advantages need not be elaborated.

4. **Drug usage or cost reports**

   Because drugs dispensed or used are entered daily in the records concerned by the computer itself, retrieval of information about drug usage is easily carried out. Similarly, the cost of those drugs can be calculated without many efforts. These details are required by hospital management for the efficient hospital administration. Thus computers are of great use in hospitals.

5. **Billing**

   Though drugs are given free of cost to the patients in government hospitals, it is charged in private hospitals. Hence, preparing bills for the drugs and other items supplied to each patient is an important function for pharmacists. Using a computer, bills are easily generated and sent to the hospital accounts department and also given to the patients.

6. **Patient profile**

Patient medication profile is prepared using hospital/ dispensary computers and updated then and there so that they can be used during the patient's subsequent visit to the hospital. It also helps the doctors and clinical pharmacists in monitoring or modifying therapy. Without storing this information in computers, it will be much more difficult, time-consuming and confusing to do those works manually.

7. **Drug therapy Monitoring**

It requires complete data about the patients and their current therapy, previous medication history, allergy etc. They are obtained from the patient medication profile, and patients are monitored for any drug-related problem, progress or otherwise of the treatment, and the results are conveyed to the doctor concerned.

8. **Drug therapy problems and management**

Drug interactions, Adverse drug reactions, Ineffective drugs and other problems in the treatment are detected by clinical pharmacists and recorded. Then those problems are either solved or managed in consultation with treating doctors, nurses and other people concerned. If severe, these problems are reported to higher authorities of the hospital, State Drugs Control department, and National Pharmacovigilance centres through computers in the form of electronic records.

9. **DUR / DUE Reports**

In modern hospitals where clinical pharmacy services are established, Drug Utilization Review [DUR] or Drug Use Evaluation [DUE] are undertaken periodically to find out the correctness of the treatment. They are carried out by the entire healthcare team involved in the treatment. It is also one of the regular works of the Therapeutic committee of the hospital, The review or evaluation details are entered into the computers of the hospital and communicated to the higher authorities. It is nearly impossible to maintain such voluminous data manually without a computer. Reports are prepared at the end of this exercise using a computer for accuracy, clarity and follow-up actions.

10. **Preparation, use and maintenance of Hospital Formulary**

This is dealt with elsewhere in this book in detail. A bulk volume like a Hospital formulary cannot be prepared or used, or maintained easily without computers. Though it is prepared once in a few years, revision is done then and there frequently, otherwise, the hospital formulary will not serve its purpose. Needless to point out, it is easier using a computer than doing it manually. Thus uses of computers in hospitals are crystal clear.

11. Drug information Centre

The organisation, functions and maintenance are explained in detail in a separate chapter. Collecting, storing and retrieving required information in a few minutes are possible only with a computer. Internet offer immense possibilities that thousands of websites are assessed in a few seconds, and needed information can be obtained from them using computers. That apart, Databases of various topics are also available in DVD formats and are used to get needed information within a short time and supplied to information seeker wherever he is. It is unthinkable without a computer in Drug Information Centre.

12. I.V. Admixture and TPN detail

These are specialised works assigned to pharmacists by doctors. The work requires accuracy, reliability and sincerity in preparing I.V. admixture and Total Parenteral Nutrition. Computers are of enormous help in that work. Also, the detail stored in pharmacy computers helps in future reference and follow-up.

Thus computers in hospital pharmacy practice not only make a pharmacist's work easier but also brings appreciation to him if used properly.

Electronic Health Records [EHR]

Data about the health aspects of the patient or population at large are stored in computers electronically, and they are known as Electronic Health Records [EHR]. At the patient level Medication profile is a significant record maintained on the computers of hospitals or community pharmacies. It acts as a complete record with detail about the patient's past and present health conditions, including diagnosis, allergy, and surgery underwent. It can also be extended to record his immunisation status. If not all, important prescriptions given to the patient are also stored.

On the other hand, health records of the society are maintained electronically by the government regarding morbidity, mortality, immunisation, family planning and other particulars. It helps the government in planning healthcare projects and budgets.

In September 2013, the Government of India notified the Electronic Health Record standards. It was revised later in the year 2016. These standards specify the particulars to be collected from the people starting from the demography and patient identifier to digital certificate. The notification also explains the need for Electronic Health Records as follows:

"For a health record of an individual to be clinically meaningful, it needs to be from conception or birth at the very least. As one progresses through one's life, every record of every clinical encounter represents a health-related event in one's life. Each of these records may be significant or insignificant depending on the current problems that the person is suffering from. Thus, it becomes imperative that these records be available, longitudinally arranged as a time series, and be clinically relevant to provide a summary of the various health care events in the life of a person."

Thus, an electronic health record is a collection of various medical records that get generated during any clinical encounter or event.

Advantages of EHR

WHO lists the following advantages of Electronic Health Records.

1. It improves the accuracy and quality of data entered into the health record.
2. Enhance health care practitioners assess to patient's health care information enabling it to be shared by all for the present and continuing care of that patient.
3. Improve the quality of care as a result of having health information immediately available at all times for patient care.
4. Improve the efficiency of the health record service
5. It contains health care costs. In future, a paperless environment will come.

Software used in Hospital Pharmacy

There is much software available for use in Hospital Pharmacy. Out of the two important categories of it, one is for the distributive function, another for Clinical pharmacy activities in a hospital.

Distributive application software includes prescription processing for both community and hospital pharmacies. Clinical pharmacy software has clinical applications like Therapeutic Drug Monitoring [TDM], Biomedical Research models, Drug interaction screening, ADR detection and prevention, dosage calculation support for I.V. admixture and TPN. Advanced software is now available, which helps in medical decisions in infectious diseases and cancer. There are scores of software available for retail pharmacies. Some of them are Holemind, Medicine ERP, Red book, Medoz, Logic ERP and Medeil. Some other software includes Abacus Pharmacy software, PioneerRx, WinRx and Good Rx.

Questions

Short Answer Questions

1. List a few areas where the computer is used in Hospital Pharmacy
2. What are the advantages of Electronic Health Records?
3. Name a few software used in retail pharmacy

Long Answer Questions

4. Explain a few uses of computers in Hospital Pharmacies with examples
5. Write in detail about Electronic Health Records
6. Enumerate the use of computers in Hospital drugs store and Drug Dispensary

CHAPTER 10

CLINICAL PHARMACY

Definition

Clinical pharmacy is defined as a system concerned with rational selection and use of medicaments at the patient level to ensure the patient's maximum well-being while on drug therapy.

Scope of Clinical Pharmacy

Though clinical pharmacy services are yet to be introduced on any large scale in India, it is very well practised in developed countries, and their scope is wider. Starting from Drug information to doctors, health care professionals and people, it extends to getting patient medication history, ward round participation, treatment care review, ADR monitoring and patient counselling. Thus, its scope is bigger and broader. All these clinical pharmacy services are explained in detail below.

Development of Clinical Pharmacy in India and Other Countries

Before studying the development, first, we must know the origin and the reason for the development of clinical pharmacy services. The immediate reason for the evolution of the concept of clinical pharmacy was the THALIDOMIDE disaster of 1960-1961. The drug Thalidomide was developed in West Germany and marketed in several countries. It was given for controlling nausea and vomiting during the early stages of pregnancy and was available without the requirement of a prescription as an OTC drug.

However, Thalidomide given to pregnant women produced 'PHOCOMELIA' – an arrested development of limbs of newborn infants. In West Germany alone, there were 10,000 birth deformities. The drug also affected thousands of infants in other countries such as England, Israel, Australia, Belgium, Brazil, Canada, East Germany, Egypt, Lebanon, Peru, Spain, Sweden and Switzerland, totalling a few lakhs babies.

The thalidomide disaster has been a terrible lesson to the world, which shocked the entire healthcare team. On analysing the disaster, it was found that new drugs were introduced into the market in haste without proper scientific studies after administration to human beings. Hence the process of introducing new drugs was lengthened and tightened. Also, it was found that generally, there is no one to monitor the effects of drugs, especially the adverse reactions of a drug on the human body after administration of a drug. Hence the concept of clinical pharmacy evolved, in which the pharmacist is given the responsibility of monitoring the drug's action after administration to the patients.

Though this service was introduced in those countries a few decades back, it is yet to be started in India. In the last decade Pharmacy Council of India made efforts to prepare manpower, -- the first requirement to start the service – by introducing a six-year degree programme by the name 'Pharm.D' in pharmacy colleges. Now we have dozens of pharmacy colleges offering this course, and hundreds of Pharm.D graduates are passing out every year.

However, they are yet to be appointed as Clinical Pharmacists in our hospitals. Few big private corporate hospitals appoint and utilise their services to a certain extent. Many deemed universities, having medical colleges and hence teaching hospitals under their control, started Pharm.D courses and offer clinical training to those students in such hospitals. Thus, manpower is ready in India for clinical pharmacy services, but not the place to serve!

The development of clinical pharmacy services in India largely depends on two factors. 1. Acceptance and appreciation of these services as helpful by medical practitioners. 2 Demand by patients and the general public. The former is very important because there is a wrong notion prevailing among doctors that clinical pharmacists interfere in their work. Hence doctors are reluctant -- even opposing – the appointment of Clinical Pharmacists in hospitals. This wrong opinion about clinical Pharmacists must first be removed by demonstrating how useful their services are. For this, forerunners who are now in clinical pharmacy services should be exemplary and prove the benefits to the doctors through their works, writings, publications and propagating their achievements in all forums.

Once doctors realise it, they themselves will demand and establish these services in our hospitals. Also, the service will be introduced if we create demand by educating the general public about the need and benefits of clinical pharmacy services. If the patients come to know what they are losing in the absence of clinical pharmacy services, they will start demanding it. The very important point which should be focussed on them is the absence of monitoring of drug's activity in their body to prevent drug's side effects. That apart pharmacist should establish the fact that he alone is suitable for the job as no one else is studying all about drugs, including their chemical, physical, pharmaceutical and pharmacological properties. Also, the facts that he alone is taught to formulate, manufacture and analyse the drugs. Other courses, including medical, nursing, or physiotherapy, do not teach these subjects, which must be emphasised. Eventually, clinical pharmacy services will be introduced in India.

Technical Definitions and Common Terminologies

Introduction

A pharmacist in clinical settings needs to understand the medical abbreviations and terms used by clinicians, nurses and other health care professionals. Hence, he must have a fair knowledge of those words and thereby be able to understand whatever is discussed during ward duties and other occasions. He has to use, interpret and apply these words while performing his duties. This knowledge can be acquired fast only in practical settings, and hence he should spend more time in wards and Outpatients Department rather than in Drug Information centres or Medicine Stores or Dispensaries during his training.

Though pharmacists have some basic understanding of medical terms through the subjects they have studied, like, Anatomy, Physiology, Biochemistry and Pharmacology, they are insufficient in a hospital arena where a team of health care professionals are practising. Hence, he must try to learn these terms as much as possible. It may not be possible to list all the medical and technical terms here as it is very large and requires hundreds of pages. Hence only very important terms with their meanings, which are often used, are given here. Students are advised to have a standard pocket medical dictionary in their coat pocket while undergoing training and refer to it then and there to understand the language spoken by their trainers or until they gain experience. They should learn to speak quickly in professional language with the members of the health care team.

These terms are available on scores of websites on the internet, like popular Wikipedia, medicine plus, quizlet, med lexicon etc., and hence what is required is initiative and willingness to learn.

Significance of Medical Terminology

Only when a pharmacist understands the meaning of medical terms used in clinical settings, he can serve better. For example, the terms like paediatrics, geriatrics, antenatal care, and postnatal care refer to the specific category of patients and the services to them should also be specific and as per instructions. The following are a few **technical and common terms** used in clinical settings.

Pediatrics: Pediatrics is the branch of medicine dealing with the health and medical care of one-day infants to 18-year adolescents. The word is coined from two Greek words, pais = child and iatros = healer, meaning thereby healer of children

Geriatrics: A branch of medicine that deals with the problems and diseases of old age and the medical care and treatment of ageing people. Gerontology is the study of ageing, including biological, sociologic and psychologic changes.

Antenatal care: It is also known as Prenatal care. According to the National Health Mission of the Government of India, Antenatal care is the systemic supervision of women during pregnancy to monitor the progress of foetal growth and to ascertain the well-being of the mother and the foetus.

Postnatal care: It is otherwise called as Postpartum care. It is defined as the care given to the mother and her newborn baby immediately after the birth of a baby and for the first six weeks of its life. It is to help with postpartum recuperation and restoration.

Autopsy: It is also commonly known as a post-mortem. It is defined as the examination of the body after death to determine the cause of death. Post-mortem is the Latin word meaning 'after death'

Morbidity: Morbidity or morbidity data refers to the proportion of people in a specific location that is subject to illness and disease. The morbidity rate refers to the number of people affected by a particular disease.

Mortality: It is the number of deaths in a particular population. It is expressed as number of deaths per 1,00,000 population.

Premedication: Generally used only of drugs given in preparation for anaesthesia.

Prognosis: The likely outcome or course of a disease; the chance of recovery or recurrence

The following are the medical terms:

ABSCESS	–	SWELLING DUE TO COLLECTION OF PUS
ACUTE	–	SEVERE, SUDDEN
ACROPACHY	–	CLUBBING OF FINGERS AND TOES
ACUTE MYOCARDIAL	–	HEART ATTACK INFARCTION
AFEBRILE	–	WITHOUT FEVER
AMBULANT	–	ABLE TO WALK
AMENORRHOEA	–	ABSENCE OF MENSES
ANGINA	–	CARDIAC PAIN DUE TO POOR BLOOD SUPPLY TO HEART

ANOREXIA	–	LOSS OF APPETITE
ANOXIA	–	WITHOUT OXYGEN
APNOEA	–	CESSATION OF BREATHING
ARTHRITIS	–	INFLAMMATION OF JOINT
ARTERIOSCLEROSIS	–	THICKENING OF LUMEN OF ARTERIES
ARRHYTHMIA	–	ABNORMAL CARDIAC RHYTHM
ATAXIA	–	AN UNSTEADINESS OF BODY/MUSCLES
AURA	–	A VISUAL DISTURBANCE BEFORE EPILEPTIC FIT
AZOOSPERMIA	–	ABSENCE SPERM IN SEMEN
BACTERIURIA	–	PRESENCE OF BACTERIA IN URINE
BRONCHITIS	–	INFLAMMATION/INFECTION OF LUNGS
BRADYCARDIA	–	SLOW HEART RATE
CARCINOMA	–	A MALIGNANT NEW GROWTH
CHOLECYSTECTOMY	–	REMOVAL OF GALL BLADDER
CIRRHOSIS	–	LIVER DAMAGE [SHRUNKEN AND HARDENED]
COLIC	–	ACUTE ABDOMINAL PAIN OR PERTAINING TO COLON
CONCUSSION	–	LOSS OF CONSCIOUSNESS DUE TO SEVERE HEAD INJURY
CRYPTOGENIC	–	OBSCURE OR DOUBTFUL ORIGIN
CRYSTALLURIA	–	EXCRETION OF CRYSTALS IN URINE
DECUBITUS	–	LYING DOWN
DEMENTIA	–	MENTAL DETERIORATION OF FUNCTIONS
DELIRIUM	–	MENTAL DISTURBANCE MARKED BY HALLUCINATIONS
DERMATITIS	–	INFLAMMATION OF SKIN
DIMORPHIC	–	APPEAR IN TWO FORMS
DISTAL	–	AWAY FROM CENTER
DYSCHEZIA	–	DIFFICULT OR PAINFUL EVACUATION OF FAECES
DYSPAREUNIA	–	DIFFICULT OR PAINFUL INTERCOURSE
DYSURIA	–	DIFFICULT OR PAINFUL URINATION
DYSPNEA	–	DIFFICULTY IN BREATHING

DYSPHAGIA	–	DIFFICULTY IN SWALLOWING
ENURESIS	–	INVOLUNTARY DISCHARGE OF URINE
EMPHYSEMA	–	A LUNG DISEASE WITH LOSS OF LUNG TISSUE [IN SMOKERS]
ENCEPHALOPATHY	–	ANY DEGENERATIVE DISEASE OF BRAIN
EPISTAXIS	–	BLEEDING OF NOSE
FEBRILE	–	PRESENCE OF FEVER
FISSURE	–	ANY CLEFT OR GROOVE
GASTRITIS	–	INFLAMMATION OF LINING OF STOMACH WITH PAIN
GASTRO ENTERITIS	–	INFLAMMATION OF STOMACH AND INTESTINE [WITH VOMITING]
GLAUCOMA	–	INCREASE IN INTRAOCULAR [EYE] PRESSURE
GLOSSITIS	–	INFLAMMATION OF TONGUE
GLYCOSURIA	–	LARGE AMOUNT OF SUGAR IN URINE
GONORRHOEA	–	A CONTAGIOUS INFECTION OF GENITAL ORGAN
HAEMOTEMESIS	–	VOMITING OF PURE BLOOD OR WITH STOMACH CONTENT
HAEMOTOMA	–	WELL DEMARCATED BRUISE
HAEMATURIA	–	BLOOD IN URINE
HAEMOPTYSIS	–	COUGHING UP OF BLOOD
HAEMORRHAGE	–	BLEEDING [INTERNALLY OR EXTERNALLY]
HEMIPLEGIA	–	PARALYSIS OF ONE SIDE OF THE BODY
HEPATITIS	–	INFLAMMATION OF LIVER
HYPERGLYCEMIA	–	HIGH LEVEL OF SUGAR IN BLOOD
HYPOGLYCEMIA	–	LOW LEVEL OF SUGAR IN BLOOD
HYPOTHERMIA	–	LOW BODY TEMPERATURE
INCONTINENCE	–	LOSS OF CONTROL OF URINARY BLOODER OR BOWEL
INTUBATION	–	INSERTION OF TUBE

ISCHEMIA	– LACK OF BLOOD SUPPLY TO HEART
KERATITIS	– INFLAMMATION OF CORNEA
KETONURIA	– EXCESS OF KETONE BODIES IN URINE
LEUKEMIA	– BLOOD CANCER
LIBIDO	– SEXUAL DESIRE
LUMBAGO	– PAIN IN LUMBAR REGION
	– AN ELATED OVERACTIVE STATE OF MIND AND BODY
MENORRHAGIA	– EXCESS AND PROLONG BLEEDING AT REGULAR INTERVALS OF MENSES
MENINGITIS	– INFLAMMATION OF MENINGES [MEMBRANE AROUND BRAIN]
MYALGIA	– PAIN IN MUSCLES
MYOPATHY	– UNEXPLAINED MUSCLE WEAKNESS OR SORENESS
NAUSEA	– FEELING OF VOMITING
NEURITIS	– INFLAMMATION OF NEURAL TISSUE
NECROSIS	– DEATH OF TISSUE
	– A MENTAL CONDITION WITH ANXIETY etc.,
NOCTURIA	– WAKING AT NIGHT TO PASS URINE
OEDEMA	– FLUID COLLECTION IN TISSUES [SWELLING]
OTOTOXIC	– TOXIC ACTION ON EAR
OSTEOARTHRITIS	– DEGENERATION OF CARTILAGE OF BONE JOINTS
OSTEOMALACIA	– DECALCIFICATION OF BONES [DUE TO LESS VITAMIN D]
OOPHORECTOMY	– REMOVAL OF OVARY
PALLIATIVE CARE	– CARE TO MINIMIZE PAIN NOT CURE
PALPITATIONS	– A RAPID AND IRREGULAR HEARTBEAT
PARAPLEGIA	– PARALYSIS OF LEG OR LOWER PART OF BODY

PROXIMAL	–	NEAREST TO CENTER
PANCREATITIS	–	INFLAMMATION OF PANCREAS
PARKINSONISM	–	IMPAIRMENT OF MOVEMENT, RIGIDITY AND TREMOR
PARANOIA	–	A PSYCHOLOGICAL DISORDER OF DELUSIONS
PEDICULOSIS	–	INFESTATION OF SKIN [SCABIES]
PHLEBITIS	–	INFLAMMATION OF VEIN
PHOBIA	–	AN IRRATIONAL FEAR
POLYDIPSIA	–	EXCESSIVE THIRST PERSISTING FOR LONG TIME
PNEUMONIA	–	INFECTION OF LUNGS
POST PARTUM	–	AFTER CHILDBIRTH
PROGNOSIS	–	LIKELY MEDICAL OUTCOME OF DISEASE
PSYCHOSIS	–	AN EXTREME DERANGEMENT OF MIND
PSYCHOSOMATIC	–	NERVOUS COMPLAINT WITH BODILY SYMPTOMS
PULMONARY EMBOLUS	–	MOBILE BLOOD CLOT IN LONG TISSUE
RHINITIS [ALLERGIC]	–	NASAL CONGESTION, DISCHARGE & SNEEZING
RHEUMATISM	–	INFLAMMATION AND PAIN IN JOINTS
RETINOPATHY	–	ANY NON-INFLAMMATORY DISEASE OF RETINA
SCHIZOPHRENIA	–	A NERVOUS DISORDER DISTURBING NORMAL THOUGHT PROCESS
SYNDROME	–	A GROUP OF SIGNS & SYMPTOMS DUE TO DISEASE
SENILE	–	RELATING TO CHARACTERISTIC OF OLD AGE
SEPTICEMIA	–	PRESENCE OF BACTERIAL TOXINS IN BLOOD
SPASM	–	CONVULSIVE, INVOLUNTARY MUSCULAR CONTRACTION
TACHYCARDIA	–	INCREASE IN HEARTRATE ABOVE 100/MINUTE

THROMBOCYTOPENIA	–	DECREASE IN NUMBER OF PLATELETS
URICOSURIC	–	TENDENCY TO INCREASE THE EXCRETION OF URIC ACID
VARIOLA MINOR	–	A MILD SMALLPOX
XEROPHTHALMIA	–	LACK OF TEARS, DRYNESS OF EYE DUE TO VITAMIN. A DEFICIENCY
XEROSIS	–	DRY SKIN

Daily Activities of Clinical Pharmacists

1. Ward Round Participation

Introduction

A medical practitioner going round the ward of the hospital where his patients are admitted for review or follow up of the treatment given to each patient, either alone or along with his junior doctors and other members of health care team is known as ward round. This is undertaken either daily or at fixed time intervals depending on the need and rules of the hospital.

Usually, only chief or senior doctors goes on a ward round with his assistant doctors, house surgeons or interns and medical students. Assistant doctors who are actually involved in treating the patients get advice and suggestions from the senior or chief doctor regarding the treatment and make many visits to the ward on a single day with or without somebody accompanying him.

Thus, the chief doctor's visit to the ward acquires significance when the entire healthcare team is available for taking instructions and/ or for consultation.

Goal of Ward Rounds

During ward rounds, doctors are provided with valuable information on different formulations, their strength, availability, side effects, suitability for the particular patient, alternative or substitute drugs etc., on the spot by clinical pharmacists. That is to say, that information is given when it is needed most, that is, at the time of prescription writing for the in-patients. Thus, he helps the medical practitioner to *ensure the safe and rational use of drugs and thereby improved patient care at less cost and time.* That are the goals of ward rounds.

Procedure for ward round Participation:

Preparation for Ward Round by Clinical Pharmacist

A clinical pharmacist needs to get ready before the ward round by the chief doctor of the ward. He may have to advise or suggest or offer consultation regarding the medicines prescribed for the in-patients of the ward. For which he has to prepare and keep ready the following:

1. Medication profile of each patient
2. Summary of medication history of each patient
3. Summary of Drug Utilization review
4. Recommendation he indents to make based on the above documents and
5. Supportive documents and references for the above.

In spite of the best care by the entire health care team, there is still a possibility for drug interaction, adverse drug reactions and medication error. Drug- Diet interaction, Drug- Diagnostic test interaction, and Drug-Disease interaction are the three DDs, a clinical pharmacist needs to watch, as other types of reactions are mostly avoided by the treating team by careful planning and monitoring.

Patient Medication Profile are maintained in all the hospitals where clinical pharmacy services are available. A clinical pharmacist has to keep it updated and ready for ward rounds.

During the discussion regarding the selection of drugs for the patient, his medication history is very much useful. Hence at least its summary, if not the full history, must be available for reference by the treating clinician. The history is not only useful while prescribing immediately after diagnosis but also during the course of treatment, depending on the patient's response or otherwise for the drugs administered. This factor makes it an important document till the patient's discharge.

If Drug Utilization Evaluation [DUE] has been undertaken on a particular patient by the DUE team and its report is communicated to the treating team, a copy of it must be ready with the clinical pharmacist. It helps to go for course correction in light of recommendations made by the DUE team.

Finally, a clinical pharmacist should prepare beforehand if he indents to make any recommendation or suggestion to change a drug or its dose or addition of another drug etc. He should able to cite relevant references for his recommendations so that the treating clinical practitioner accepts it without any hesitation or doubt.

All the above homework by clinical pharmacists ensures better treatment for the patient and appreciation for his services.

Pharmacist Interventions

There are many contributions and few interventions a clinical pharmacist has to make during ward rounds. The clinical pharmacist has his own limitations in that he is an authority only on drugs and related matters.

Hence as far as possible, he should not and need not interfere with the diagnosis, pathology and aetiology of diseases. However, that does not mean he should not raise his doubts or the toxic effects manifestations of the drug on the patient. He should be ever vigilant while watching for ADR or Drug interactions and report his observations to the treating clinician.

In many hospitals where clinical pharmacy services are fully established, he is empowered to order investigative lab tests to confirm the drug's toxicity. If the results of these tests confirm his suspicion, he can boldly intervene in the treatment process, equipped with test results from the lab. Thus, a clinical pharmacist's intervention should be, as far as possible, based on solid evidence. Subsequently, such interventions are welcomed and appreciated by the healthcare team. After gaining the confidence of the chief doctor and his team in this way, his future doubts and observations will be given due attention in future, even before lab results.

Pharmacist's Contribution during Ward Rounds

Most of the time, a clinical pharmacist's contribution during ward rounds will be on matters relating to drugs. Doctors, nurses and medical students may require the following information on the spot; without they resort to referring books or websites:

1. Formulations [Dosage forms],
2. Dose
3. Indications and Contraindications
4. Drugs availability and its supply source
5. Economy [price]
6. Substitute [if the above is not available]
7. Time required for getting the supply
8. Legal and administrative issues and
9. Special storage conditions, if any.

If the clinical pharmacist is able to give this information immediately, without referring to any book or source of information, his value and respect among the team peaks and a fruitful team spirit develop. This results in the better name for the hospital.

Completion of Ward Round

Having discussed what to do before and during the ward round, let us discuss what to do after the ward round. During the preparation for the ward round clinical pharmacist update and keep ready the medication profile of the patient and related documents like medication history, DUE and DUR documents and other documents. After the ward round is completed, he has to update these documents with additional information discussed and decided during the latest ward round. This information is noted briefly in a hand-held case diary during ward rounds and elaborately written in the registers of the clinical pharmacy department.

Before attending to this work, the clinical pharmacist must give priority to the information if he has promised to give his team members. They may be urgently required by the team members to complete their records or to commence the follow-up treatment decided during the ward round. If no such work is there, he can attend to the updating work as discussed above. Thus, documentation is one of the major works after the ward rounds.

Next, he can communicate the decisions to other departments concerned, if relevant and necessary. He may have to communicate with hospital administration, the Head of Nursing Services, the Head of Pharmacy services, the Head of Lab services and the Head of dietary services. This information may be sent via e-mail or in writing, or through phone, as the case may be. Acknowledgements, if required, can be collected from them through messengers and filed.

Finally, the clinical pharmacist has to communicate some of the decisions like changes in therapy, drug or procedure to the patient or his caregivers. This has to be done carefully while counselling the patient. Thus, patients are encouraged, and their cooperation is ensured to continue the treatment. Some part or entire work of this nature is assigned to nurses also. In that case, the clinical pharmacist has to brief the nurse concerned about matters related to clinical pharmacy services before such patient counselling sessions.

2. Treatment care review

Definition

Treatment care review is a process by which a clinical pharmacist reviews the patient's treatment regimen to ensure effective, safe and economical therapy.

Needless to say, it is the responsibility of the clinical pharmacist to ensure the best therapy possible for each patient. To do that effectively, a Clinical Pharmacist must be knowledgeable in pharmacokinetics, pharmacodynamics, therapeutics, ADR, lab data analysis and clinical reasoning. All these require information from various sources, and he must be able to interpret and utilize them properly. He should carry out this review daily for complicated cases and periodically for other cases. He must be ready with this review before participating in the ward round along with treating physicians.

Purpose of Treatment care Review (TCR)

The prime purpose of TCR is effective, safe and economical therapy for all patients. However, by undertaking TCR, a clinical pharmacist is able to identify

(a) Patients who are in need of counselling

(b) Patients who require special attention and

(c) Patients with the risk of medication error.

To achieve these purposes, the TCR must be broad-based and multi-component in nature. They are discussed below:

Scope of TCR

Treatment care Review (TCR) is a broad function of which Therapeutic Drug Monitoring (TDM) is one of the components. In order to perform TCR, the clinical pharmacist needs to prepare pre hand. TCR is actually the review of the entire therapy of the patients with drugs. Hence, to arrive at a correct conclusion, a clinical pharmacist should know the previous and present condition of the patient. He has to assess the treatment goals and how far and how best it is achievable. He must be sure whether the present therapy is proceeding on the correct line to achieve the set goal.

It may not be easy for complicated cases and sometimes difficult even for cases with manageable problems, as there are many chances of patients developing complications during the course of treatment. For example, there could be drug-related problems like non-responsiveness to the standard drug regimen, sub-therapeutic dose, overdosage, and adverse drug reactions, including drug-drug interaction, drug-food interaction or drug-disease interaction.

Hence therapeutic drug monitoring (TDM) by body fluid analysis or pharmacokinetic studies should be carried out wherever necessary. Using the data obtained from TDM, the dose of the drug should be individualized, and a correct regimen arrived at.

Thereafter again, the therapy must be monitored closely in order to find out the treatment outcome. Thus, the scope of TCR extends from patient medication history to TDM and beyond.

Duties Involved in TCR

As indicated above, the first and foremost duty involved in TCR is collecting as much information about the patient's previous and present condition. This includes collecting information about patient's past medical history, including prevailing diseases before the present illness and treatment undertaken or undergoing, allergy or sensitivity to drugs, habits, daily routines etc. Along with the above detail, present condition, treatment and clinical progress or otherwise will lay the foundation for drug therapy review.

This information can be gathered from various sources, like patient's medication history interview, laboratory results, nursing notes, observational charts and case sheets. As described elsewhere in this book, the value of a medication history interview is well known that it not only reveals almost everything about a patient's present and past problems, but it also helps in finding etiology or reasons for the present problem and for arriving at a correct diagnosis and drug regimen. An interview conducted by a Clinical Pharmacist can also reveal the drugs already used by the patient, especially OTC drugs, drugs from alternative systems of medicine, household remedies etc.

The next important duty in TCR is setting and evaluating the treatment target or goal. A complete cure is what patients wanted but that may not be always possible. Hence a realistic target must be fixed like reduction of severity of disease, elimination of signs and symptoms of disease, slowing advancement of disease etc. The treatment goals are obviously patient-specific and vary patient to patient due to patient's age, weakness or susceptibility etc. This target or goal of therapy should be reviewed periodically, and the progress evaluated. Suitable corrections can be made in that target and the reasons for failure analysed. For this the entire team involved in the treatment of the particular patient is consulted and involved actively in the correction process.

Another crucial duty in TCR is the identification of drug-related problems that occurred during the present therapy. If the treatment is in a hospital where clinical pharmacist's services are available, problems like inappropriate drug selection, sub-therapeutic dose or over dosages are less. However, even though these problems may occur in a few cases, hence a quick review must be carried out in these aspects also during TCR. More series problems like complications due to untreated indications or patient's multiple diseases or organ failures, adverse drug reactions that occurred during the course of treatment etc, has to be reviewed carefully.

Once the drug-related problems, if any, is identified and resolved, the next step is to correct the regimen to suit to the individual patient. This can be achieved by switching over to sustained release or once-a-day formulation, changing the route of administration, time of administration etc. While changing the regimen to suit the individual, care must be taken to maintain the cost-effectiveness of the therapy and also ensure compliance of the regimen by the patient. Multiple drug prescriptions or polypharmacy must be controlled as far as possible by including combination drugs wherever possible.

After carrying out all the duties during TCR, as detailed above, the results of the treatment must be monitored. For this, the clinical review and tests carried out by and on the instructions of the treating physician are highly useful. The laboratory data, such as the results of blood tests, x-ray, scans, liver function tests, kidney function tests, etc, can be used for the purpose of monitoring. Some drugs may produce the desired results after a fairly long time. For example, antidepressants require 30 to 40 days to produce a response in patients. However, if a drug does not produce the required result within a reasonable time, a careful review of the drug prescribed must be made. A dose increase or replacement of a drug with some other drug or addition of one more drug to the regimen may be needed.

Medication Chart Review

This is one of the important duties assigned to clinical pharmacists in developed countries in order to prevent medication errors and to ensure the best treatment possible to the patients. It has become an essential function in those countries because patients sue the doctors and hospitals for a very huge sum as compensation in the courts, if anything goes wrong during the course of treatment. As such a situation does not exist in our country but is slowly and steadily picking up, medication chart review is yet to be implemented here. However, future pharmacists need to know the process of medication chart review as these duties will also be assigned to him in India sooner or later.

Medication errors are preventable errors that may occur during prescription writing and/or drug administration. To prevent those errors, pharmacists must systematically review the medication charts. The following are the guidelines to carry out a medication chart review:

1. Poorly written, illegible prescriptions should be returned to the prescriber and checked. It should not be guessed.
2. The identity of the patient must be clear, for which the name, age, sex, hospital number etc, of the patient should be clearly written on the medication chart. If not, check and write.
3. If the patient is allergic to some drugs or tests, it should be legibly written on the space provided in the medication chart with red ink. If no allergies are reported or identified, it should also be mentioned in that place.
4. The name of the drug, dose and route of administration should be written by the treating physician, and it should be checked. No abbreviations should be used to write the name of the drug. As far as possible, generic names should be written on the chart, if not written, the pharmacist should write it next to the brand name. The dose and dosage interval should be correct and as intended by the doctor, depending on the patient's condition. Any extraordinary dose should

be underlined by him to indicate he means it. Decimals should be avoided as far as possible, as it may lead to ten times more dose if not seen. For example, it should be 5 mg, not 5.0 mg and 0.5 gm, not .5 gm.

5. The time of administration should also be mentioned in the medication chart. If it is not suitable for the particular patient, for example, if there is the possibility of Drug-Drug interaction or drug-food interaction, the pharmacist can write an annotation on the chart, recommending a change in the time of administration of the particular drug.
6. Prescriptions with instructions like SOS (as required or whenever necessary) should have a minimum dose interval to have adhered to, otherwise, there is a possibility of overdosage.
7. Additional instructions like after food, before food, with plenty of water etc., can be written by the clinical pharmacist wherever necessary.
8. The medications should be prescribed according to the legal and local requirements of the government concerned. It should be signed and dated by the prescriber, and any corrections in the medication chart should be endorsed by him.
9. The medication chart should also be signed by the nurse who administers the drug to the patient in the space provided. Thus, the medication chart will be a complete and authentic record of the treatment given to the patient.

Model Mediation Chart

XYZ Hospital

Patient name: .... IP No: .... Unit:												
Age: .... Sex: ....Height: .... Weight:												
Allergy:												
S. No.	**Name of the drug**	**Dose**	**Route**	**Time of admn.**	**Day of administration (Nurse initials)**							
					1st	**2nd**	**3rd**	**4th**	**5th**	**6th**	**7th**	**8th**
1.				8 am 2 pm 8 pm								
	Additional instructions											
	Signature of doctor with date											

Table *Contd...*

2.												
	Additional instructions											
	Signature of doctor with date											
3.												
	Additional instructions											
	Signature of doctor with date											
4.												
	Additional instructions											
	Signature of doctor with date											
5.												
	Additional instructions											
	Signature of doctor with date											

3. ADR Monitoring

Definition: ADR can be defined as a reaction that is harmful, unintended and occurs at doses normally used in humans for the prevention or diagnosis or treatment of diseases.

Goal of ADR Monitoring

It is to reduce the incidence of ADR and thereby saving the patients from the harmful effects of drugs. Though Adverse Drug Reactions cannot be eliminated, it can be reduced if the drugs are used with caution and by following the safety aspects listed below by the patient and health care team.

1. Patient medication history should be obtained before prescribing, and drugs should be prescribed accordingly.
2. Drugs should be administered only when required. If there is no indication, such drugs should not be used.
3. As far as possible, the minimum number of drugs should be prescribed. Polypharmacy or multiple drug regimens should be avoided.

4. Children and old people are susceptible to ADR. Hence, they should be monitored while under therapy.
5. Continuous review of the need for the drug should be undertaken, and the dose should be reduced or the drug altogether stopped at an appropriate time.

Procedure for ADR Monitoring

Methods of Detecting and Monitoring ADR

As it is difficult to differentiate between the disease manifestations and the Adverse Drug Reactions, many methods are developed to identify ADR. They are:

1. Case-control studies
2. Cohort studies
3. Spontaneous case reports and
4. Vital statistics and record linkage studies

1. **Case-Control Study:** In this study, groups of persons with disease (cases) and groups of persons without disease (control) are compared. Here the disease selected should be due to the drug. Patients' medication histories are collected and compared, if the drug has caused the disease, its use among the cases should be many times more than the controls.

   This type of study can be conducted quickly and effectively, and that too at less cost. But it requires more scientific knowledge to conduct correctly and to interpret the data obtained after the study.

   For example, in a study of the relationship between lung cancer and cigarette smoking, it was found the disease is 10 to 11 times more in smokers than non-smokers. As the connection between the two depends on the amount of smoking and there is very less scope for chance factor, hence the conclusion drawn from the above study is justified.

2. **Cohort Study:** A cohort is a group of people having approximately the same age and put under the same and similar conditions like receiving the same drug. In this study, the drug under study is given to the group and watched for varying periods to find out the ADR. This can be for a short period, say the treatment period plus 1 month. The study is carried out in various places in the country, and up to 2000 to 3000 patients are selected.

   Usually, toxic effects due to excessive pharmacological effects are detected by this method. Delayed effects of the drug can also be detected.

In the long-term study lasting for few years more patients up to 20,000 may be followed for detecting adverse drug reactions. Information is collected from the Doctor, Pharmacist and patient if possible. The problem with this method is dropouts due to migration etc. It is an expensive and difficult method and known as Post Marketing Surveillance.

3. **Spontaneous Case Reports:** If a prescriber suspects some problem with the patient because of drug usage, he reports it to medical or pharmaceutical journals or to the manufacturer of the drug. This is called a spontaneous case report. Other prescribers are alerted by this method.

   Nowadays, ADR reporting agencies are available like the one with World Health Organization (WHO). Once a report is sent to them with relevant particulars, they investigate and or report it to all medical practitioners through journals, newsletters and associations etc. It is a cheaper method; however, the frequency of a particular ADR, its correlation with drugs and disease etc., has to be determined. Also, it cannot be claimed to be a complete report.

4. **Vital Statistics and Record Linkage Studies:** All the health care institutions (hospitals and clinics) and local bodies are required to maintain morbidity and mortality data. From these records, diseases prevailing and causes of death in a particular area can be collected and analysed.

   However, this method is not successful because of a long delay in collecting data, the reliability of the data etc. If the data are faithfully entered into records and computerised, it may be useful to collect and analyse them easily in future.

Management of Adverse Drug Reactions – Role of Pharmacists

Irrespective of careful treatment of the patient, ADR do happen due to many factors beyond the control of the health care team. In those unfortunate events, the pharmacist has the following functions to manage ADR.

First of all, he should review the available literature regarding the ADR of the particular drug. Any worthwhile point found should be discussed with physicians. Next, the pharmacist should check the patient's medication history. He should also review other factors like co-administration of other drugs, stage of disease etc. Therapeutic Drug Monitoring (TDM) should be started immediately if not started already. The plasma concentration of the drug in the particular patient should be analyzed and weather the reaction is dose dependent or not can be detected. Finally depends on the seriousness of the reaction he can advise to stop the drug. For this he has to analyze the risk/benefit ratio and the availability of substitute drugs.

If pharmacy and therapeutic committee is available in a particular hospital, pharmacist as the secretary of PTC should inform the committee about the ADR that occurred. PTC, in turn, discusses it and advises the treating physician on what to do and how to proceed with further treatment. It monitors the recovery of the patient from ADR and ensures proper treatment thereafter. The pharmacist has to implement the decisions of PTC as its secretary.

All Records of adverse drug reactions should be preserved and reported to suitable higher authorities.

4. Drug Information and Poison Information

These topics are explained in separate chapters. Refer to Chapter No 14 & 15

5. Medication History

Definition: Medical history of a patient is a record of the patient's past medical and surgical history, including his family medical history, social history, allergy and current medications. It is obtained by inquiry or interview with the patient [or his attendant, initially] by a clinical pharmacist or doctor.

Goal of Medication history

The goal of medication history is to open the possibility for the best treatment and consequent reduction in time, energy and money involved in the treatment.

Procedure for medication history interview

Pre-requirement for an interview:

The patient who is to be interviewed by the pharmacist might have had the same or some other disease earlier, and that illness experience and the present mood bring in lot of stress on the patient. Hence, outright cooperation from the patient cannot be expected. We know that if someone is sick in our family, not only the patient but the entire family is worried and disturbed. All routine work of all family members gets disturbed if it is the breadwinner of the family got sick. These patients are more worried about expenses and loss of income than the disease itself. Moreover, they exaggerate everything in their mind and worried about permanent disability, helplessness and even death. Hence a Clinical pharmacist must be sympathetic and helpful to the patient so that he can cope with the situation. This is the most important pre-requisite for a medication history interview.

The success or otherwise of an interview depends on the pharmacist's approach. He must start the interview with as much as information about the patient in his possession. At least he must know the patient's name, age and present complaint from hospital records. Also, he should know the physical condition of the patient, like whether the patient is in acute pain, conscious and communicative. Usually, patients are admitted in the wards after first aid and other emergency or essential clinical procedures in the outpatient department (OPD). The pharmacist must verify this, and hence he can safely assume that the patient may be in a position to answer his questions during the interview. Similarly, knowing the probable diagnosis may help in providing some idea about the severity of the disease, the possible diagnostic procedures ahead etc. Thus, a thorough preparation before the interview is the pre-requirement for an interview.

Structure of Patient's Case History

What is patient's medication history and its content are discussed below in detail. Let us first summarise its structure.

- Patient's name, age, sex and address
- Date of admission and patient hospital registration number
- Present complaint
- Already existing diseases like T.B., Asthma, Diabetes etc.
- Medicines currently using [Prescription and OTC drugs with the dose used]
- Use of drugs of alternative systems medicine like Siddha, Ayurveda etc.
- Allergy to drugs, food and others
- Problems encountered, if any, during drug use [ADR, Drug Interaction]
- Immunization [if relevant]
- Pregnancy and any problem faced [if applicable]
- Any surgery undergone and its current status
- Social drug use habits [alcohol, tobacco etc.]
- Any evidence of drug abuse or misuse
- The general attitude towards medicine use [compliance/ noncompliance]
- Patient's opinion for present illness.

As mentioned earlier, all the above information cannot be obtained in one sitting by the Clinical Pharmacist, follow up may be needed to get the left-out information. For example, the patient may not remember the name of the medicine he already used for his present or past illness. That has to be gathered from his old prescriptions or discharge note, or bills of community pharmacies or by seeing unused balance medicines. Even direct contact with community pharmacists where the patient used to purchase medicines through phone may be required. By all means, the clinical pharmacist must try to get the full information listed above by clever questioning and efforts during a medication history interview. Only a complete and comprehensive interview will serve its purpose of ensuring correct, quick and cheaper therapy for the patient and help the hospital authorities to conduct an effective Drug Utilization Evaluation [DUE] later.

How to conduct a useful Interview?

The interview should be started with a polite self-introduction which leads to long time relationship and rapport between the pharmacist and the patient. Medication history interview is not an exemption to this. Clinical pharmacists must open the interview with self-introduction after verification of the patient's identity. This must be followed by defining his role as interviewer, the purpose, probable time required for the interview etc. Thus, the patient's mood is brought to normal, and he is inclined to cooperate. Then without going for specific details, his general daily routines, hobbies and his social history, like neighbourhood environment etc., can be enquired about.

Once this preliminary part of the interview is over, the pharmacist should use his communication skills to get full and correct information about his medication history. He should get details about the prescription and non-prescription medicines currently taken by the patient. He should also gather information about previous diseases or chronic diseases under treatment at present, allergies or problems with adverse effects and possible drug misuse. All this information will not be coming out straight away, hence pharmacist has to put clever questions, some may be open questions, and some may be closed questions.

Open questions are the ones for which the patient can give lengthy, descriptive answers and the closed questions are required to be answered with 'yes' or 'no'. Obviously, closed questions offer no option to the patient to avoid or circumvent the answer and hence should be used judiciously without offending the feelings of the patient. If offended, the further interview will be a waste and ends in failure as the patient's cooperation ends with his wounded personality.

Careful questioning will not lead to such an unpleasant end. Hence pharmacists must be attuned to the types of questions asked, the manner in which questions are asked and avoid repetitions. As far as possible technical terms should be avoided, and if absolutely necessary, its meaning should be explained.

Patients are always in a mental setup that once a person is willing to listen, they open up and exhaust all their problems and feelings. Pharmacists must make use of this mentality of patients to gather the needed information. He should cleverly make the patient to speak about his real body problems without much interruption.

This apart, a successful interview requires the use of correct body language by the interviewer. Body language helps in conducting a useful interview rather than using mere spoken words.

Role of Body Language

In order to communicate with others, body language plays an important role. Not only the words but also the body communicates a lot of messages to others. Communication through sign language by deaf and dumb persons is an example of this. When a message is delivered with facial expressions, hand gestures and other body movements and postures, as in cinema and drama, it reaches the receiver quickly. The pharmacist also uses it instead of sitting idle with blank looks in front of the patient.

Looking at the eyes of the patient while he speaks, head nod and inclining towards the patient are some of the signs of the body which indicate the pharmacist is actively listening to the patient. Similarly, even the voice of the pharmacist while speaking to the patient has a significant role. The tone and tempo of voice convey the message that one is sympathetic towards other or not. A voice filled with concern for the patient will definitely influence him. Thus, a sweet, empathetic voice is of great help to the pharmacist to achieve what he wants.

Role of Prompts

Irrespective of the pharmacist's sympathetic behaviour and good body language, all the needed information from the patient cannot be obtained due to various reasons. Few among them are patients' forgetfulness or lack of concentration, or ignorance about what medicine they are taking and what for. It is more acute in the case of illiterate and semi-literate patients. They may not be able to answer the pharmacist's questions accurately, as such, the medication history interview may not be useful.

In such a situation, interviewing pharmacist has to adopt a few techniques like prompting or getting help from the family members of the patient. Prompting is nothing but stimulating or leading a person to start and sustain something. Pharmacists can ask prompting questions so that the patient starts recollecting the answer for the questions. Prompting help trigger the patient's memory. For example, the pharmacist can ask do you take medicines for your hypertension. Or do you apply anything externally for any skin infection? Such questions make the patient to recollect even treatments given to him a long time back. Thus, prompting questions asked by pharmacists results in a fruitful interview. If the correct answer is not forthcoming even after prompting, the pharmacist has to rely on patients' family members or caregivers.

Interview Questions

Apart from the above, pharmacists can ask questions about new medicines given by the doctor, medicines stopped or changed by him, etc. In order to get full information, pharmacists can ask a number of questions on the use of OTC drugs mentioning the symptoms and diseases usually treated by OTC drugs. Invariably many chronic patients go to doctors of alternative systems of medicine out of their anxiety to get cures for their long-time diseases. They try to hide such treatments and medicines from the healthcare team out of guilty consciousness. They also hide their visits to many doctors of modern medicine at the same time. Only by winning the patient's faith and confidence pharmacist can bring out such truths. While questioning patients, pharmacists should ask non-biased questions and avoid leading questions like, 'you don't smoke, do you?' Leading questions prompt the patient with a particular answer.

Even pharmacists forget to ask some important questions during the interview. In order to avoid such lapses, pharmacists can follow some patterns of asking questions, such as 24-hour surveys and reviews of systems of the human body. In the 24-hour survey pattern, questions can start from the patient's life of getting up from bed in the morning to going to bed at night. Similarly, if questions are asked about body system-wise diseases or treatment, a complete interview is possible.

Sometimes even after so much preplanning and organisation, important, needed information on medicines previously and currently used by the patient cannot be obtained due to the single factor that the patient don't remember anything worth about his medicines. In such cases, the patient or his caregivers should be asked to bring all medicines–even the empty containers–used by the patient as early as possible to complete the interview. Patients should be educated to carry the list of current medications–both prescription and OTC medicines and also, they should be encouraged to purchase from the same pharmacy always by explaining its benefits.

However, information about patients' non-compliance with instructions of doctors, pharmacists and other healthcare team members is difficult to get.

Nobody admits their mistake easily. Hence clever probing questions like the following should be asked to find out non-compliance:

1. Do you carry medicines to your workplace?
2. Do you forget some doses?
3. What will you do if you forget to refill the prescription?
4. If the medicine is inconvenient to you in any way, what will you do?
5. Do you use costly medicines as and when needed or as per the doctor's instruction?
6. Have you ever increased or decreased the dose of a drug?

From the answers to these and similar questions, non-compliance, drug misuse, and abuse can be guessed, and such findings should be promptly intimated to the treating physician through the final report after the medication history interview.

Closing an Interview

To close the interview pharmacist must highlight a part or the entire interview to the patient, which permits the patient or the interviewer to correct any error, clear any confusion, confirm information already given or add new information.

At the end of the interview, the pharmacist can ask for additional information which the patient thinks might be useful. Also, he can ask the patient's opinion or reasons for the present problem. One more opportunity can also be given to the patient to make corrections, if any. All these points should be noted in a short form, then and there, during the interview itself and elaborately written immediately after the interview as a report for the reference of the treating physician and health care team.

Advantages of medication history interview

If an interview is conducted properly and all the relevant information is obtained from the patient, it helps the medical fraternity enormously. The advantages are numerous and beneficial to all the persons involved in the health care of the patient, including the patient himself. It helps in speedy and correct diagnosis. It avoids unnecessary repetitions of earlier ineffective treatment; it saves the patient from unpleasant exposure to drugs allergic to him; it prevents the patient from ADR, drug interaction etc.

It also gives an idea about the patient's habits, weaknesses and dependence or requirements. Hence clinical pharmacists can effectively monitor the drug therapy later or modify the drug therapy to suit the need or condition of the patient. Without the prior medication history of the patient on hand, these things are not possible, and it may be too late to have such data at a later stage.

6. **Patient Counselling**

Definition

Patient counselling is defined as an interactive session designed to educate and inform the patient about his medication, treatment, and expected outcome and also identifying and remove the barriers so as to lead to appropriate therapy.

Goal of counselling

The major aim of the counselling is to improve the compliance by the patient to the instructions of the health care team and to remove any barrier like misconception, fear or non-confidence in the therapy and thereby achieving the best outcome at the end of the treatment.

Introduction

Counselling is done at the end of a long course of treatment just before discharge, but that is not a hard and fast rule. Counselling can also be at the beginning or middle of the treatment, depending on the need. During the patient medication history interview, information about the patient is gathered, whereas information is given during counselling. After the diagnosis, the treating physician gives some outline about the disease suspected and probable treatment and duration. If more information is required to be given to the patient, counselling is conducted. Similarly, during the treatment, in order to ascertain the patient's feelings about his disease, its severity or comfort, problems in medicine usage etc., a counselling session is conducted.

At the end of the treatment, just before discharge, the patient is instructed about the continuation of treatment in the home, do's and don'ts regarding diet, exercise, a repeat visit to the hospital etc. This session of counselling will be worthwhile because, after discharge, the patient loses the supervision by the doctor, pharmacist and nurses and hence a careless attitude of the patient may result in a relapse of the disease or more complications.

Patients used to hide some facts or mistakes committed by them to the doctor. By counselling, a good counsellor can bring out those hidden truth by winning the confidence of patients. Thus, counselling is beneficial to both the healthcare team and patients.

Need for counselling

Counselling involves the two-way exchange of information between the pharmacist and the patient, and hence it is better than written communication. Moreover, legally and morally, pharmacists have to give information about the drugs patients use. It should be in sufficient quantity and in language the patients understand. Hence the need for counselling is obvious. Again, if the counselling has to be effective, it should be conducted in a place free from noise, interruption or distractions. If such privacy is provided, the patient will understand the importance given to it and cooperate with a counsellor. It improves the image of the pharmacist, and he will be recognised as one contributing to his welfare. Generally, the disease is a private affair of the patient hence he is hesitant to speak about it openly. When such foolproof privacy is provided, he tends to speak more about his inner problems and feelings.

Thus, fruitful counselling can be conducted when privacy is provided.

Procedure for counselling

The first step is to select the patient for counselling. Routine counselling of all patients is both impossible and unnecessary. Patients are selected according to the need. For others, a few minutes of counselling is sufficient and given during regular ward rounds or at the time of administration of drugs. Relatively long counselling sessions are needed for:

(a) Patients are to be subjected to long-term treatment e.g.: Epilepsy cases.

(b) Patients with diseases but without severe symptoms e.g.: Prophylactic cases of TB.

(c) Patients using drugs with narrow therapeutic index. e.g.: Warfarin.

(d) Patients with the danger of abrupt stopping of treatment. e.g.: Corticosteroid therapy.

(e) Patients with potential for non-compliance, abuse or misuse of drugs. e.g.: Treatment with tranquillizers.

Patient Education and Counselling

Patient counselling is nothing but a form of patient education, as a majority of information given during counselling is for the purpose of educating the patient. If it is considered as an education, then it need not be restricted to a few patients. As many patients as possible should be educated so as to achieve the best clinical outcome of the treatment.

American Society of Health-System Pharmacists [ASHP] says, "Pharmacists should educate and counsel all patients to the extent possible, going beyond the minimum requirements of laws and regulations." ASHP also emphasise, "Pharmacists should encourage patients to seek education and counselling and should eliminate barriers to providing it." Though guidelines are given above to select patients for counselling, pharmacists should try to accommodate as many patients as possible in the interest of the patient, society and his own profession, which earn respect from the patients through these services.

Patient education and counselling can be carried out in all four types of pharmacy practice, viz, Inpatient care, Outpatient care, Home care and Community care settings. However, counselling requires some prior preparation to be useful to the patient and to the institution.

Preparation for Counselling

It differs between the four settings mentioned above. If the counselling is for an inpatient at the time of discharge, needed information about the patient can be obtained from hospital records. However, if counselling is to be carried out at the time of admission of the patient or a few days after the admission or for outpatient or in community pharmacy settings, the pharmacist should gather all relevant information about the patient before starting counselling. If a pharmacist could acquire knowledge about a patient's culture, especially his health and illness beliefs, attitudes and practices, it goes a long way in dealing with him. If the counselling is done after a few days of admission and in the middle of the treatment, counselling has to be in a different plain so as the patient to realise his disease can be cured if he adheres to the instructions of the health care team. After all, every patient wants to go home earlier after curing their disease, hence getting their cooperation may not be a problem. Small complaints like frequent injections, lab procedures and big bitter tablets they start tolerating if the counselling is effectively done. Similarly, outpatients will realise that whatever the doctor, pharmacist or nurse told them was for their welfare after brief counselling. Hence for the counselling to be successful, the pharmacist should get himself ready for it.

As there is no effective supervision of the patient after discharge, proper counselling is needed to prevent relapse and readmission of the patient. Appropriate learning aids like graphics, anatomical models, medication devices, memory aids, printed pamphlets and audio-visual resources should be kept ready in the counselling room. Whichever aid is needed must be used to boost the level of understanding of the patient, if necessary, by demonstration.

This apart, while getting ready for counselling, the pharmacist should review the discharge prescription and ensure a clear medication list and instructions for discharge. The patient's follow-up plan should also be ready. As mentioned above, a fairly good idea about the patient to be counseled can be collected from hospital records. The patient may be a child or aged patient or mentally ill, or terminally ill patient. Depending on the type of patient, the pharmacist has to plan his counselling content. For example, counselling a child's prior idea about its level of understanding is important. On the other hand, an elderly patient may be vision or hearing impaired, a terminally ill patient may not be interested in counselling at all and may not listen, and the mentally ill may not understand and co-operate with counselling. Before counselling, a pharmacist must prepare to face all the above situations.

Scope of Counselling or Contents of Counselling

The scope or purpose of patient counselling is for giving instruction and motivation to patients and monitoring them. The counselling for outpatients differs from counselling for inpatients. To inpatients, certain points like how to open or administer drugs, timing and amount of dose etc., need not be discussed, as they are taken care of by nurses. Those instructions need to be given only at the time of discharge, along with storage conditions, refill information etc. However, all this information has to be conveyed to outpatients, along with possible side effects, what to do if one or two doses are missed and the duration of treatment. For complicated regimens like multiple drug regimens or sophisticated or complex packings, drugs have to be shown to the patient and explained. This not only makes them understand better but also helps the pharmacist in the detection of dispensing or prescription errors. A few words about the use and importance of each drug will lead to better compliance and consequent success of treatment.

Moreover, patients may be interested in knowing the expected duration of treatment and expected benefits. They can be briefly mentioned while discussing the importance of adhering to the instructions. Possible drug-drug interaction and drug-food interaction should be informed. The technique of self-monitoring of treatment should be taught to the patient. Depending on the patient's disease management and therapeutic plan, some education can be given regarding the disease state, its effect on normal life and the identification of disease manifestations.

Before closing the counselling, session patient may be encouraged to speak his mind regarding the treatment. This is very important because they have many unanswered questions, misunderstandings and problems which they may not reveal to the healthcare team. In the absence of answers to these problems, they make their own decisions regarding the treatment. Only when they are prompted do they tend to open up and ask questions and share their experiences with treatment.

After clearing the patient's doubt pharmacist can ask a few questions at the end to estimate the patient's level of understanding and knowledge about counselling points. If required, the pharmacist can once again clarify his doubts with materials and demonstrations. At any point in time, the pharmacist should not assume that the patient has understood all the information given and think that if there is a problem, he will contact him. Also, he should not assume that someone else in the health care team—a doctor or nurse—might have already told everything to the patient while he was in the ward.

Effect or uses of Counselling

Due to Counselling,

1. Knowledge of disease and its treatment among the patients improved.
2. Patient compliance improved.
3. Repetition of drugs already under use or used can be avoided.
4. Pharmacist contribution towards disease documentation increased.
5. Since compliance improved, disease aggravation reduced.
6. Because of it, emergency visits to hospitals or hospitalization or subsequent expenses are reduced.

Thus, counselling plays an important role in disease management. Hence clinical pharmacists should be appointed in all Indian hospitals.

7. Inter-Professional Collaboration

Introduction

A pharmacist's public relations and professional relations are important aspects of pharmacy practice. Pharmacist, by virtue of their job, has to move with many professional colleagues in the hospital and outside. They are doctors, nurses, lab technologists, research scholars, drug suppliers and their representatives. Also, outside his pharmacy field, he may have to move with other professionals like clerical, administrative, maintenance and other staff like drivers, transporters and even load men! He should learn and master such works, so us to be successful in his profession.

1. **Professional Collaboration with the medical and nursing staff**

   American Society of Health-system Pharmacists [ASHP] has published a guideline for the collaboration of pharmacists and nurses in institutional care settings. They are relevant to hospitals of all countries and hence discussed below:

   True and sincere collaboration by way of professional relations among pharmacists and nurses reflects in the quality of patient care. The complexity of drug treatment requires this collaboration between nurses and pharmacists on a regular basis. Pharmacists, on their part, can supply drug information to the nurses, on the other, nurses can provide valuable information on the effect of drugs on the inpatients, as they are directly involved in patient care.

   The orientation programs for the students and newly appointed nurses or pharmacists can be reciprocal in that orientation for nurses disseminate information about various services provided by the pharmacy, and the program for student pharmacists can include an introduction to a patient care unit [ward] and its functions by nurses. Professional collaboration should be there whenever the roles of professionals [pharmacists and nurses] overlap. For example, in the area of inpatient education, monitoring ADR, ward rounds and in nursing care plans, both these professionals can cooperate and exchange information and observations.

Nurses equipped with adequate drug information and knowledge of patients are in a better position to administer the drugs properly at the correct time, dose and frequency and detect undesirable drug effects, if any. On his part, a pharmacist should provide the following drug information in adequate level and extend to the nurses:

1. Information on new drugs.
2. Information on investigational drugs used in the hospital.
3. Probable side effects and therapeutic risks of the drugs prescribed.
4. Contraindications to particular drug therapy.
5. Compatibility and stability of drugs, including I.V. admixture.
6. Drug dose calculations, if any.
7. Essential pharmacokinetic data about the drugs prescribed.
8. Possible drug interactions [Drug-Drug, Drug-Food and Drug-lab tests] and
9. Effect of patient's age and disease on drug's action.

Apart from the above, pharmacists should record information that is important to the patient's medication regimen in the patient's record. Specific allergies to drugs should be highlighted on the patient's record. As discussed elsewhere in this book, nurses should be supplied with pharmacy newsletters or bulletins and the latest edition of the hospital formulary, all prepared by hospital pharmacists. All the above information and services can be given to junior doctors especially to resident doctors [house surgeons] who are in direct contact with patients in wards.

Clinical pharmacists, by participating in ward rounds with doctors and nurses, can review patient medications. A fruitful exchange of information and discussions among Physicians, Pharmacists and Nurses results in better therapy, speedy recovery and discharge of the patient, and that is the goal of the health care team.

2. Professional Collaboration with research staff

Though clinical research is carried out by exclusive Clinical Research organisations [CRO] established for the purpose of research, hospitals also play an important role in research activities. CROs have their own limitation in that they cannot have human volunteers of all varieties, and all diseases cannot be artificially induced in them, hence big hospitals with varieties of patients and varieties of diseases are unavoidable in research activities.

Research can be undertaken for new drugs or new indications for old drugs, as well as on drugs suspected of ADR. In all these researches, a pharmacist can provide needed background information gathered through the hospital drug information centre to the research staff. An extensive research literature survey is possible only through Drug Information Centre, as it has all the primary, secondary and tertiary sources of information.

If needed and requested, formulations can be prepared and supplied by pharmacists using the raw materials given by research staff. Moreover, a pharmacist, as a person in charge of stores of the hospital and procurer of raw materials for the hospital drug manufacturing unit, can arrange an inventory of investigative materials for the research staff.

3. **Professional Collaboration with medical reps and suppliers**

Medical representatives are the people who supply the latest information about drugs and formulations newly introduced in the market. Thus, they are considered as part of the educational program and objectives of the hospital. Hence a pharmacist has to develop appropriate rapport with them so that hospital staff starting from the pharmacist himself, will benefit from his specialised knowledge.

Most of the time, these representatives are considered as interruptions in the busy work of pharmacists and physicians, and hence not much time is allotted for his detailing and display materials. It is a wrong approach on the part of hospital staff, especially for pharmacists, as pharmacists are required to gather and give drug information to the staff, which is being readily supplied at his desk by the medical representatives. Thus, a medical representative is helping the pharmacist in his job, so he must be provided with quality time and attention.

In order to do that properly, time must be allocated for the visit by a medical representative every week or fortnight as required. They must be encouraged to adhere to that time schedule, and their genuine concern regarding the allotted time should be addressed. Fixing prior appointment avoid embarrassment and/or disappointment for both parties. But its success lies in adhering to or honouring the appointment by both of them.

Medical representatives supply drug or product information through literature and samples. Pharmacists should collect them and forward them to the physicians and members of PTC for getting approval for future purchases. While medical representatives make a presentation or detailing, pharmacists must make a note of it in the product information sheet, model of which adopted from William Hassan is given below:

PRODUCT INFORMATION SHEET

NAME OF THE PRODUCT...

MANUFACTURER..

GENERIC NAME..

ADDRESS..

CHEMICAL NAME..

SYNONYM...

COMPOSITION [IF IT IS A FORMULATION]	THERAPEUTIC USE OF EACH INGREDIENT
....	....
....	....
....	....
....	....
....	....
....	....
....	....
....	....

INDICATION........................ CONTRAINDICATION..............

TOXICOLOGY........................ ANTIDOTE.............................

DOSAGE & ADMINISTRATION ----- DOSAGE FORM ----- EQUIVALENT PRODUCT

....	....
....	....
....	....

PACKING AND PRICE LITERATURE: YES/ NO

.... SAMPLES: YES/ NO

DATE:..................... PHARMACIST'S SIGNATURE....................

SPACE FOR PTC'S OPINION / RECOMMENDATION:

....

....

The above form is submitted to the PTC during its agenda for product approval for the purchase and its inclusion in Hospital Formulary. Thus, in an institutionalised modern hospital pharmacy, a pharmacist's professional relationship with medical representatives and drug suppliers goes long way in providing better treatment for the patient with the latest drugs.

In the hospital with PTC and modern hospital pharmacy set up and control over the freedom of doctors in prescribing drugs [only those listed in the hospital formulary has to be prescribed], even samples given by medical representatives has to be used only after approval by PTC. Hence these samples are supplied to the hospital stores only, not to the individual doctor in the ward or OPD. As with other drugs, a physician has to order these samples through prescription to the patient and the same is dispensed by the pharmacist. Hence the list of samples available with dispensaries or stores will be periodically circulated to the doctors. Thus, the use of drugs by a patient of the hospital is completely under the control of PTC.

Thus, there are many daily activities for a clinical pharmacist to perform in a hospital. This apart, a few other duties are assigned to them once in a while, like Pharmaceutical care, Medication therapy management, ADR management for particular patients etc. They are described in separate chapters.

Questions

Short Answer Questions

1. Define clinical pharmacy.
2. Define Pediatrics and Geriatrics
3. What are Antenatal care and post-natal care?
4. What is the goal of the Treatment care review?
5. List 4 methods of monitoring ADR
6. Why is patient counselling required?

Long Answer Questions

7. Explain the need or concept of clinical pharmacy.
8. Write an essay about ward-round participation by a pharmacists
9. Explain the method of Medication history interview

10. Briefly explain the importance of inter-professional collaboration.
11. Explain the role of the Pharmacist in Treatment care review
12. Detail the patient counselling procedure.

CHAPTER 11

PHARMACEUTICAL CARE

Introduction

Pharmaceutical care is a new concept that evolved during the middle of the 1970s after pharmacists were given the responsibility of monitoring drug therapy in the 1960s. It is an extension of Clinical Pharmacy services and developed into a full scheme of pharmaceutical care. Many of the functions assigned under this concept are new to pharmacists, and hence a section of them was reluctant to accept those responsibilities. These works involve not only monitoring, reviewing and documenting the therapy but also taking full responsibility for the result.

Definition

Helper and Strand have defined "Pharmaceutical care as the responsible provision of drug therapy for the purpose of achieving definite outcomes that improve a patient's quality of life."

FIP adopted the above definition with little modification. They inserted the words 'or maintain' after the word 'improve', and thus the new definition is,

"Pharmaceutical care is the responsible provision of drug therapy for the purpose of achieving definite outcomes that improve or maintain a patient's quality of life."

It is obvious that in certain disease conditions like AIDS or Diabetes, improving a patient's quality of life is not always possible. Just maintaining it at the present level of quality, without further deterioration, itself considered as a significant achievement.

***Pharmaceutical care and clinical pharmacy*:** The above definition looks similar to the definition of clinical pharmacy services. What is the difference between them? Roger Walker says, 'the practice of clinical pharmacy is an essential component in the delivery of pharmaceutical care.' He further elaborates, 'the delivery of pharmaceutical care is dependent on the practice of clinical pharmacy, but the key feature of care is that the practitioner takes responsibility for a patient's drug-related needs and is held responsible for that commitment. Thus "pharmaceutical care is a cooperative, patient-centred system for achieving specific and positive patient outcomes from the responsible provision of medicines", he concludes. From the above quote, it is clear that in pharmaceutical care pharmacist takes direct responsibility for the patient's drug-related needs and thereby assures its quality in this care.

***Types of Pharmaceutical care*:** As per the above definition pharmacist takes full responsibility for the drug therapy given to an individual patient under the concept of pharmaceutical care; immediately, the question arises of who is responsible for the therapy given to the community as a whole under special circumstances. Here too, pharmacists should provide pharmaceutical care. In this population-based pharmaceutical care, he has to use demographic or epidemiological data for serving the needs of society. According to a document published by WHO, it includes establishing hospital formulary, developing and networking pharmacy services, conducting and evaluating drug utilisation reviews, developing and educating drug-related policies, etc. On the other hand, the first type of pharmaceutical care given to individual patients involves monitoring drug therapy and modifying it if necessary. Though pharmaceutical care is provided in cooperation with the entire healthcare team, the pharmacist alone is responsible for the cost, quality and outcome of pharmaceutical care.

Basic Concept of Pharmaceutical Care

1. In pharmaceutical care, first, the pharmacist plans individualised drug therapy for the patient. It aims at specific results and is formulated in consultation with other healthcare professionals and patients.
2. For the above plan, evidences are collected, its merits and demerits are studied and then adopted for implementation.
3. The patient is educated about the plan and its method of execution and
4. While the patient is under therapy, the outcomes are constantly monitored and modified if required.

Thus, pharmacists, in cooperation with other healthcare professionals and patients, design, implement and monitor a therapeutic plan that produces definite outcomes for the patient. These works are nicely presented by Helper et al. in their paper "Opportunities and responsibilities in pharmaceutical care", published in 1990 in the American Journal of Hospital Pharmacy.

Pharmaceutical Care, for whom?

Though it is ideal to provide pharmaceutical care for all patients, it is not possible in practice. Hence patients should be selected on the basis of the following situations.

- Patients in critical conditions or diseases, that is, patients with cardiac problems, hypertension, diabetes, asthma etc., should be given priority.
- Patients whose body conditions are vulnerable to adverse reactions, such as patients with liver or kidney damage, pediatric and geriatric cases etc.
- Patients who are given risky drugs which are sure to cause damage if wrongly used. E.g., Anticancer drugs, Aminoglycosides, anticoagulants etc.
- Patients in acute conditions and when the drugs given do not produce the desired level of therapeutic action, as in certain infectious diseases and severe diarrhoea.

When provided with pharmaceutical care, these risky patients can be saved with the cooperation and efforts of the entire healthcare team. Though the pharmacist plan, executes and monitors the pharmaceutical care program, he has to ensure the support and active participation of the full healthcare team to achieve the definite outcome planned.

Principles and Practice of Pharmaceutical Care

In 1995 American Pharmacists Association [APhA] has published 'the principles of practice for pharmaceutical care' to guide the concept of pharmaceutical care when it was started developing. In that document, it is pointed out what is needed to achieve the goal of pharmaceutical care and the various steps involved in it. The following are the excerpts from the document:

To fulfil the objectives of pharmaceutical care,

- Pharmacists must establish a professional relationship with patients and maintain it.
- Patient-specific medication information must be collected, organised, recorded and maintained.
- The above information must be evaluated, and a drug therapy plan must be developed mutually with the patient.
- The pharmacist assures that the patient has all supplies, information and knowledge necessary to carry out the drug therapy plan and
- The pharmacist reviews, monitors and modifies the therapeutic plan as necessary and appropriate in concert with the patient and health care team.

Steps Involved in the Practice of Pharmaceutical Care

1. ***Data collection:*** By medication history interview with the patient, if it is not possible—with the patient's caretakers, old medical records, leftover

medicines etc., patient-specific data is collected first. This data must be complete and comprehensive in all aspects. All these data are recorded accurately and confidentially. It is shown to others only with the permission of the patient or if required by law.

2. ***Data Evaluation:*** After evaluation, some decisions can be taken from the above data, like the opportunity to improve the present condition, the effectiveness of planned therapy, way to reduce future drug-related problems etc. These decisions can be conveyed to the patient, to the extent necessary, in order to make him understand his present condition and future prospects.
3. ***Designing a plan:*** Then, the pharmacists should design a plan to treat the patient with a specific achievable goal. For this, he can consult other healthcare professionals and enroll on their cooperation. Drugs suitable for the patient should be selected next, and ways of monitoring their effect must be identified. The design can also include non-drug treatment, dietary changes etc. It also should be clear about the therapeutic endpoint and monitoring limitations.
4. ***Executing the plan:*** The plan evolved as above should be implemented with care. During this stage, the pharmacist requires the support and involvement of other healthcare professionals, patient attendants and, of course, the patient himself. All the supplies starting from drugs to other items in time, should be ensured by the pharmacist.
5. ***Monitoring the plan and outcome:*** The pharmacist has to regularly monitor the outcome of the treatment to determine whether satisfactory progress is there or not. If it is not satisfactory, the plan should be modified and then implemented. While monitoring, the therapy patient's vital parameters should be checked using lab tests wherever and whenever necessary. However, costly tests should be avoided as far as possible to keep the cost of treatment minimum and affordable to the patient, as that is also one of the goals of pharmaceutical care. If positive outcomes are noticed, they should be conveyed to other healthcare professionals to elevate their confidence in the treatment plan. All these developments should be recorded in the patient's case diary or record so that follow-up will be more effortless. Always patients' medical and/or pharmacy records should be kept updated. Communications with other healthcare providers also should be recorded.

Requirements for Successful Pharmaceutical Care

American Pharmacists Association has listed the important requirements for the successful implementation of pharmaceutical care. They are,

1. Knowledge, skill and function of personnel

2. Systems for data collection, documentation and transfer of information
3. Efficient workflow processes
4. References, resources and equipment
5. Communication skills and
6. Commitment to quality improvement and assessment procedures

If all these requirements are in place while implementing the program of pharmaceutical care, better results can be achieved to improve the quality of a patient's life.

Evaluation of Pharmaceutical Care Services

Any product or service provided to the society should be evaluated for its quality; pharmaceutical care is not an exemption. The quality of any service, including health care services, can be assured by evaluating its structure, process and outcome. On completion of this evaluation, shortcomings, if any, can be rectified, and thus it serves to achieve a better patient outcome. The evaluation or quality assurance process starts with a focus on the patient, the process and then the result. As described above, the patient-specific plan must be prepared and implemented with the cooperation of the team. The result obtained is evaluated in the light of set goals. The quality of pharmaceutical care can be assured if the resources or structure are properly mobilised, and the plan is correctly executed.

Questions

Short Answer Questions

1. Write a note on the principle and practice of Pharmaceutical care.
2. What are the requirements for successful Pharmaceutical care?
3. List the steps involved in the pharmaceutical care process

Long Answer Questions

4. Define Pharmaceutical care. How is it carried out? Explain.
5. Describe the concept of pharmaceutical care.

CHAPTER 12

MEDICATION THERAPY MANAGEMENT AND HOME MEDICATION REVIEW

Definition

There are many definitions for Medication Therapy Management [MTM]. One definition is "MTM is the service provided by the pharmacist to optimise the response to medications for the management of treatment-related medication problems or complications."

The American Pharmacists Association defines "MTM is a distinct service or group of services that optimise therapeutic outcomes for individual patients."

Goal: The aim or Goal of MTM services are intended to address issues of polypharmacy, preventable adverse drug events, medication adherence and medication misuse. It is for improving outcomes by helping people to understand their health conditions and the medication used to manage them.

In MTM, pharmacists interview patients, identify and prioritise medication-related problems, develop and implement interventions, and document the activities. By MTM, pharmacists ensure optimum therapeutic outcomes for targeted beneficiaries through improved medication use, reducing the risk of adverse events.

In the United Kingdom, MTM is generally called Medicine Use Review. That review includes providing education on the disease state and medications used to treat the disease, ensuring that medicines are taken correctly, reducing waste due to unused medicines, looking for any side effects and providing education on how to manage any side effects. According to popular Wikipedia, in MTM, pharmacists review all the prescribed medications, any over-the-counter medications and all dietary supplements an individual is taking. This allows the pharmacist to look for any duplication or dangerous drug interactions. This service is especially useful for people who are older, have several chronic conditions, take multiple medications or are seen by multiple doctors.

The MTM is necessary for the following group of patients. 1. Those who are taking high-risk medicines 2. Those who are recently discharged from the hospital with changes to their prescribed medicines 3. Patients with Asthma or Chronic Obstructive Pulmonary Disease [COPD} 4. Cardiac patients who are given multiple drugs.

Home Medication Review

Definition

Home Medication Review [HMR] is a service offered by pharmacists to the patients who are under treatment at their homes instead of hospitals where pharmacists verify, monitor and manage the drug regimen prescribed by the doctors and thereby prevent or correct any medication error or problem faced by the patient.

It is a consumer focussed service given to patients by pharmacists on the advice of treating physicians or at the request of patients themselves. It is very much in practice in developed countries and slowly picking up in India among the patients who can afford to pay for it.

Need for HMR

Home Medication Review may not be required for all patients who are undergoing or continuing treatment in their homes. It is needed in the following situations:

1. Patients who are taking multiple drugs [Polypharmacy]
2. Patients with complex drug schedules
3. Patients who continue or want to continue other systems of medicine simultaneously for the same disease or coexisting other disease.
4. Patients who are noncompliers with instructions given and
5. When there is a likelihood of Adverse Drug Reactions.

Aim of HMR

HMR is aimed at Improving compliance by patients by identifying the reasons for non-compliance. Once non-compliance is corrected automatically, it leads to the improvement of the patient's quality of life and, ultimately, to cure of his disease. It also increases the patient's knowledge about his medication, and thereby chance for medication error and ADR is reduced to a larger extent.

Method of HMR

There are many steps involved in undertaking HMR. The first step is to identify the patient for HMR. In other words, we must select the patient for whom HMR is required as obviously it is not required for all patients continuing treatment at their home.

1. Patients who are taking more than five regular medicines or 12 doses of medicines per day or being treated for a minimum of 3 medical conditions.
2. Patients whose medicines are changed significantly in the recent past.
3. Those who are taking drugs with a narrow therapeutic index or requiring TDM
4. Non-responsiveness or sub-therapeutic response to the standard drug regimen
5. Suspected non-compliance or symptoms of ADR
6. Risk due to language or literary barriers
7. Patients are taking treatment simultaneously from different doctors and/or different systems of medicine.
8. Geriatric or pediatric cases with eyesight or cognitive function failures or without proper helpers.

The second step, after the identification or selection of a patient for HMR, is the assignment of HMR work to a recognised pharmacist by the treating physician or hospital. The pharmacist thus selected must be provided with all relevant information about the patient's clinical condition and other detail.

The third step involved in HMR is obtaining patient consent and subsequent cooperation from the patient concerned. The fourth step is conducting an HMR interview with the patient. It is, by and large similar to the medication history interview described elsewhere in this book. The outcome of the interview is the identification of noncompliance, medication errors, the potential for ADR, improper dose, unnecessary medication, untreated indication, improper use of medical devices and other wrong practices by the patient.

The fifth step in the process, as expected, is that the results or observation by the pharmacist should be informed to the treating physician or hospital in the proper format, and all relevant information gathered during the interview should be conveyed with proper detail about the patient, drug regimen prescribed, date and time of interview.

The sixth step logically is to correct the mistakes or inadequacies noted during the interview. Necessary actions are taken, and counselling for the patient is carried out to carry forward the treatment. In the seventh and final step, follow-up monitoring of the patient is done so as to verify adherence to the plan of treatment.

In all the above steps, the pharmacist and the entire health care team, including doctors, should follow the laws, including consumer rights, confidentiality and privacy, and above all, consent from the patient.

Advantages of HMR

The advantages need not be emphasised here as they are apparent and self-evident. The major noteworthy advantage is benefits accruing not only to patients but to the society too, as the patient may not repeat his visit to the hospital, thereby reducing the burden on the doctor, hospital and the government. Though HMR is time-consuming and stressful for the healthcare team, it is worth undertaking.

Questions

Short Answer Questions

1. Define Medication therapy management
2. What are the goals of Medication therapy management
3. What is Home Medication Review?
4. Write the need for HMR.
5. List the advantages of HMR.

Long Answer Questions

6. Write in detail about Medication therapy management
7. Write an essay about Home Medication Review
8. How to select a patient for HMR?
9. Write the aim and need for HMR.

CHAPTER 13

LABORATORY TESTS

Patient Laboratory Tests -- Significance

In hospitals, clinical laboratory tests are carried out on many patients. The results of those tests are very much useful in the diagnosis, prevention and treatment of diseases. However, in order to arrive at a decision, a reference standard is essential. This reference is usually available in the form of the quantitative range, which is obtained by testing normal disease-free individuals.

The primary duty of a clinical pharmacist is to individualise the dose and drug regimen of the patient, for which he has to rely upon pharmacokinetic data, as well as routine haematological data. Hence, he should possess at least a working knowledge of the significance of lab tests. Using that knowledge, he has to evaluate the outcome of the treatment so far given and recommend to the treating physician the changes to be made in the drugs or doses or treatment itself.

Also, depending on these results, he has to determine the appropriateness of the treatment, the efficacy of the treatment and also the drug's toxic effect, if any occurred. Thus, lab tests play a significant role in safe and effective therapy.

Lab Tests Interpretation

While interpreting the results of lab tests, one has to be careful in that they are always not reflecting the true condition of the patient. If anyone of such a parameter is in excess of the range, it does not mean the person has got a disease. Similarly, if it is lower than the range, that is also not indicative of any series problem with the patient. All these data have to be viewed along with other signs and symptoms. There are many individual variables also, like age, sex, weight, body mass, disease etc., that affect the results of these laboratory tests. Hence, a series of tests are to be carried out before arriving at a conclusion and to eliminate errors.

Fluid and Electrolytes Balance

Fluid and electrolytes are the important components of any living organism, and they have to be in constant concentration and in balance so as for the body to function properly. The self-regulatory, feedback-controlled stabilisation of the body as a whole or any sub-system like fluid and electrolytes balance is known as Homeostasis—[Homeo – of similarity, Stasis – stopping the flow]. Water or fluid, electrolytes and acid-base balance are interrelated, and the kidney plays an important role in their balance.

Let us discuss what disturbs their balance, what happens when they are in excess or less, and steps to be taken to restore their balance, etc., in this chapter.

Water: Human body has a lot of water, that is, up to 50 to 60% of total body weight is water. It is required to maintain body temperature and metabolic reactions. They are the vehicles to carry solutes from one part of our body to another part of our body. It is distributed as intercellular fluid [ICF] and extracellular fluid [ECF] at the ratio of 2:1. That is, about 28 litres of water is present in ICF and 14 litres in ECF. The ECF is further classified into interstitial fluids [10.5 lit] and intravascular fluid or plasma [3.5 lit]. The body regulates this balance by controlling water input and output.

Regulation of water intake: We drink 0.5 to 5 lit of water per day depending on the climate and habit. This, apart from our solid food, also contains some water. They are together called as exogenous water and are mainly controlled by the thirst centre present in the hypothalamus. It is stimulated whenever the water level in our body goes down below the optimum level. Some amount of water is produced in our body itself by metabolic reactions, which is known as endogenous water, and about 100 ml is produced like this.

Regulation of water output: Water is excreted by the kidney via urine, skin via sweat, lungs via exhaled air and GI tract through faeces. Out of these four, urine is the primary source of elimination of water. About 1 to 2 litre of urine is excreted every day, and it is controlled by vasopressin or antidiuretic hormone [ADH] secreted by the pituitary gland. The secretion of this hormone, in turn, is regulated by the osmotic pressure of plasma. The skin excretes about 400 ml to 450 ml of water through sweating which depends on climate [Temperature and Humidity]. Lung excretes water through exhaled air, almost the same amount as skin, i.e., 400 ml daily. Loss of water through the GI tract via faeces is estimated to be around 150 ml per day, and needless to say, it is many times more in diarrhoea. Excess or less water intake or output leads to overhydration or dehydration, respectively.

Overhydration: It is the retention of water in the body due to excessive intake of water, kidney failure or abnormal production of antidiuretic hormone [ADH]. This may lead to headaches and even convulsions. It is treated with hypertonic saline solution and complete stoppage of water intake until the patient recovers.

***Dehydration*:** It is more common than loss of fluid during diarrhoea, dysentery and Cholera. There is loss of water from the body after a fire accident [burns] and in excess vomiting or sweating. Usually, in these conditions, not only body water is lost, but also the electrolytes Na^+, K^+ etc. Dehydration is characterised by less urine output, shrunken cells of the body due to the excretion of water even from intercellular space and increased protein destruction. Protein and urea concentrations are thus increased in the blood. Clinical symptoms of dehydration are low BP, increased pulse, sunken eyeballs etc. Usually, dehydration is treated with oral rehydration salt [ORS], where plenty of water is given orally. If it is not possible for any reason, 5% glucose or Normal Saline or Glucose saline injections are given intravenously.

Electrolytes

Electrolytes are inorganic salts which undergo dissolution in solution and exist as positively and negatively charged ions in an animal body. For example, Sodium Chloride dissociates into Na+ [cation] and Cl^- [anion]. They are measured in milliequivalents [mEq/l]. Number of grams of a substance required to combine or displace one gram of hydrogen is known as 'milliequivalents weight', and also its one-thousandth part is known as milliequivalents. It is calculated by the following formula:

$$\text{mEq/l} = \frac{\text{mg per liter} \times \text{valency}}{\text{Atomic weight}}$$

To maintain osmotic and water balance, electrolytes are well distributed in body fluids. As the electrolytes are in the form of anions and cations, they must be in equilibrium to maintain electrical neutrality.

To describe the electrolyte balance, we need to understand some words like osmolarity and osmolality, which are used to explain the concentration of these molecules. Osmolarity is about moles or millimoles of electrolytes per litre of solution. On the other hand, osmolality measures the solute present in a fluid. It is defined as moles or millimoles per kg of solvent. If the solvent is pure water, there is no difference between osmolarity and osmolality. But obviously, body fluids are not pure water and have many constituents, like proteins. Hence osmolality is invariably used to describe the concentration of molecules.

The electrolytes are important for the proper functioning of cells. It has to be balanced not only in ECF but also in ICF because the ratio between them is essential. Though this ratio is critical, their mechanism is very complex. We study mainly the concentration of electrolytes in the plasma, but to get a true picture of them, we need to go for some ancillary studies also. For example, certain electrolytes like calcium and phosphate are present in hard tissues like bone and teeth.

Osmolality of Plasma, ECF AND ICF

Electrolytes are not equally distributed between ECF and ICF. For instance, Sodium is the major cation of ECF and Chlorides and bicarbonates are its anion. On the other hand, Potassium is the predominant cation of ICF, and phosphates and sulphates are its anions. Only water moves freely between cells, but electrolytes require an active transport mechanism for its movement between cells. Though electrolyte concentration differs between ECF and ICF, their osmolarity is equal.

The osmolality of plasma is measured by an osmometer, and it is from 285 to 295 milliosmoles per kg. Sodium and its anions are major contributors [up to 90%] for this osmolality of plasma.

Balancing Electrolytes

Electrolytes are balanced mainly by three hormones, Aldosterone, Antidiuretic hormone and Renin angiotensin and also by food intake. Aldosterone increases sodium reabsorption, which increases the osmolality of plasma. This, in turn, stimulates the hypothalamus to release ADH, which on its part, increases water reabsorption. Thus, all these hormones are interrelated and function in coordination to maintain normal fluid and electrolyte balance. Rennin angiotensin regulates the flow of aldosterone in this complex process.

Our body's requirement of electrolytes is usually met by a balanced diet. During the summer months, we may need to support our bodies with extra electrolytes. The normal range of these electrolytes and water is given in the following Table.

Normal Values of Electrolytes

Electrolytes	In serum	In urine
Sodium	135 -155 mEq/L	150 – 197 mEq/ day
Potassium	3.9 -5.6 mEq/L	20 -64 mEq/ day
Calcium	8.8 -10.2 mEq/L	--
Chloride	95 – 106 mEq/L	180 – 270 mEq/day
Total anions	154 mEq/L	--
Total cations	154 mEq/L	--

Estimation of Electrolytes

Body fluids are analysed for the estimation of electrolytes using various instrumental methods. Flame photometry, x-ray fluorescence, Atomic absorption spectrometry and colourimetric techniques are used in the identification and estimation of anions and cations in the body fluids. Recent advanced methods determine both anions and cations simultaneously. Normally sodium and potassium in serum are estimated either by Flame photometry or specific Atomic absorption spectrometry. Chloride is determined potentiometrically using silver–silver chloride pH electrodes. Calcium in urine or serum is estimated by the EDTA method of analysis, or Atomic absorption spectroscopy or Flame photometry. Magnesium is measured by the ion-specific electrode, and trace elements like copper, zinc and iron are determined by flame photometric or colourimetric methods.

Uses of Study of Electrolyte Balance

The study of electrolyte balances is a useful indicator of renal and cardiac failure, anuria, adrenal cortical insufficiency, and excess electrolyte excretion. Pancreatic cystic fibrosis is detected by an excess of chloride ions in the perspiration of patients. Thus, the study of electrolyte and water balance is useful as a valuable diagnostic tool. As the analysis of metabolic excretion rates are carried out in these studies, it is useful to evaluate the functions of various organs like the liver, kidney, thyroid and other glands, which are dealt with elsewhere in this chapter.

Disturbance of Electrolyte Balance

Severe excess or less of electrolytes in the body leads to various disorders/ diseases. They are indicated by many clinical symptoms and are treatable. The cause of disturbed balance of electrolytes are many and outside the preview of this chapter, however, as a Clinical pharmacist is concerned with the effect of drugs which may be the reason for such conditions, they are listed here in a tabular form.

Effect of Drugs on Electrolytes Balance

Condition	Sodium	Potassium	Calcium	Phosphates
Excess	Hypernatraemia	Hyperkalaemia	Hypercalcaemia	Hyperphosphataemia
Symptoms	Muscle weakness, confusion, etc.	Asymptomatic but fatal	Seen in Malignancy and Renal transplantation	Seen in renal failure, Hypo para thyroids
Possible causative drugs for excess	Phenytoin, Methyl Dopa, oral Contraceptives, Clonidine, Corticosteroid, etc.	Digoxin, Isoniazid, Tetracycline, NSAID, Cyclosporine, Penicillin, etc.	Lithium, Tamoxifen, Diuretics, etc.	All drugs causing kidney damage
Less [Deficient]	Hyponatremia	Hypokalaemia	Hypocalcaemia	Hypophosphataemia

Table *Contd...*

Condition	Sodium	Potassium	Calcium	Phosphates
Symptoms	Nausea, Confusion, Drowsiness, etc.	Muscle weakness, Hypotonia, Depression, Confusion, etc.	Seen in Pancreatitis, Liver disease, Kidney disease, Vitamin D deficiency, etc.	Muscle weakness
Possible drugs responsible for deficiency	Diuretics, Heparin, NSAID, Tolbutamide, Amphotericin, Miconazole, etc.	Aspirin, Corticosteroids, Gentamicin, Insulin, Laxatives, Salicylates, etc.	Phenytoin, Phenobarbitone, Aminoglycosides, Furosemide, etc.	All drugs causing kidney damage

Haematological Tests

Among the tests performed on a patient, a blood test is the one which helps the physician more than any other test. The characteristics of blood cells and other components give the first line of diagnostic features about the diseases, deficiencies or defects that affect the human body. Hence a Clinical Pharmacist must be thorough with these tests.

1. ***RBC count*:** The normal range of Red Blood Cells in males is 4.4 to 6.1 $\times 10^{12}$/L and 4.0 to 5.5 $\times 10^{12}$/L in females. If it is less, the condition is called anaemia, and if excess, it is known as hypoxia. Anaemia may be microcytic due to iron deficiency or macrocytic due to folic acid and vitamin B_{12} deficiency.
2. ***Reticulocyte count*:** It should be 0.5% to 1% of RBC. In haemorrhage and haemolysis, it goes up to 40% of RBC. Reticulocyte count is useful to evaluate the response of bone marrow to iron, folate, and vitamin B_{12} therapy.
3. ***Mean Cell Volume* (MCV):** It is average volume of single red cell. It is measured in Femto litres (10^{-15} L). If the MCV is low, it is known as microcytic MCV, and if it is high called as macrocytic MCV. The former MCV is due to a deficiency of iron, and the latter is due to folic acid deficiency.
4. ***Packed Cell Volume* (PCV):** It is the ratio of the volume occupied by red cells to the total volume of blood. Normal value is 45%. Nowadays, it is calculated by multiplying MCV and RBC. PCV is decreased in anaemia, haemolysis and haemorrhage, whereas it is increased in polycythaemia. Obviously, it is altered in macrocytosis and microcytosis.
5. ***Mean Cell Haemoglobin Concentration* (MCHC):** It is a measure of the average concentration of Haemoglobin in 100 ml of red cells. It is measured in grams/lit or as a percentage. The normal value is 315 to

345 g/L. If it is low, iron deficiency anaemia is the reason, and if it is on the higher side, severe, prolonged dehydration is indicated.

6. ***Haemoglobin*:** It is one of the important measurements in blood tests. It differs depending on sex, a man has more Haemoglobin than a woman due to the presence of more RBC and menstrual loss, respectively. The normal value of men is 13.5 to 17 g/dl and a woman is 11.5 to 16.5 g/dl. Less than these values indicate anaemia.
7. ***Platelets* (Thrombocytes):** It is formed in the bone marrow. If it is synthesised less in bone marrow or destructed after formation, less number is seen in blood analysis. As it has a short life of only 8 to 12 days, it is easy to evaluate drug-induced thrombocytopenia (less number). It comes back to a normal level once the drug is stopped. Less number of platelets may also be due to pregnancy, viral infection or bleeding. An increased number is seen in Malignancy and inflammatory diseases. The normal value of the platelet is 150 to 450 × 10^9/l.
8. ***White Blood Cells* (Leucocytes):** This is one of the very important blood components, and its character and count in blood tests reveal a lot of information about the condition of the patient. There are two types of WBC, namely Granulocytes and Agranulocytes (Lymphocytes). Granulocytes are further subdivided into monocytes and polymorphonuclear granulocytes, which consist of neutrophils, basophils and eosinophils. Usually, WBC is measured and reported as Total Count (TC) and as differential Count (DC), which lists the number of various types of polymorphonuclear granulocytes.
   - (a) ***Neutrophils*:** They form the majority of white cells. The normal range is from 50% to 70% of total white blood cells. If it is more, there may be inflammation or tissue damage in patients, on the other hand, if it is less, it indicates malignancy or hepatitis.
   - (b) ***Basophiles*:** It is less than 1% of white cells. Its function is not clear. However, it is found less in malignancy conditions.
   - (c) ***Eosinophils*:** The normal value of Eosinophils is less than 6% of TC. It is increased in allergic conditions like asthma, Hay fever, drug sensitivity and malignant diseases.
   - (d) ***Monocytes*:** It forms 0% to 7% of total white cells. They are increased in infections like TB, typhoid etc.
   - (e) ***Lymphocytes*:** It is mainly found in the spleen and other lymphatic tissue. However, it is present in large numbers next to neutrophils in the blood. The normal value is 20% to 40%, increase in viral infections like Infectious hepatitis decreased in AIDS, Renal failure and cardiac failure.

9. ***Erythrocyte Sedimentation Rate*** **(ESR):** ESR is a measure of the sedimentation rate of red cells in a sample of blood containing an anticoagulant over a period of one hour in a cylindrical tube. The normal value is less than 10 mm/hr. It is increased in rheumatoid arthritis, inflammatory bowel diseases, malignancies and infections.

10. ***Bleeding time*:** It is the time taken by the blood to stop from the bleeding wound. It shows the haemostatic efficiency of the blood. Normally blood should stop within 2 to 5 minutes. It is increased in thrombocytopenia, platelet disorders and prolonged use of aspirin and anticoagulants. Hence clinical pharmacists should take care of these conditions of the patient.

11. ***Whole blood clotting time*:** It is the time taken by the blood to clot when tested outside the body (*in vitro*). The normal range is 4 to 9 minutes at 37°C. Prolonged time indicates haemophilia or factor 8 deficiencies or the presence of anticoagulants.

12. ***Prothrombin Time*** **(PT):** It is the time required to clot citrated plasma to which an optimum amount of thromboplastin and calcium has been added. The usual prothrombin time is 12 to 15 seconds. The PT is usually indicated as a ratio known as the International Normalized Ratio (INR), which is the ratio of PT of the patient and the normal (disease-free) man. The result of oral anticoagulant therapy can be monitored using PT. Also, it is useful to evaluate liver function.

13. ***Blood sugar*:** Blood sugar level is an important parameter that is usually checked for patients. A fasting blood glucose level of 70 to 110 mg/dl is considered normal. It is usually increased in diabetes. However, it cannot be confirmed by this elevation alone as other conditions like severe nephritis, pancreatic disease, hyperthyroidism and certain liver diseases also increase blood sugar levels. Hence glucose tolerance test [GTT] should be done on the suspected cases. 50 gm of glucose is given to the patient. Blood sugar level reaches a maximum within a short while and should return to normal within one hour 30 minutes to 2 hours. If it is not, and more than 50% in excess of fasting sugar level, it confirms diabetes. Similarly, low sugar levels indicate hypopituitarism, cretinism or hypothyroidism.

14. ***Serum enzymes*: *Alkaline Phosphate*** **ALP (or) AP:** It is present in the liver, bone, intestinal wall and placenta. Each of the above sites produces specific isoenzyme of AP. Normal range of AP is 30 to 90 IU/L. It is increased in jaundice, osteomalacia, and rickets and has low absorption of vitamin D and calcium. It is decreased in low phosphate conditions of the body.

15. ***Creatine Phosphokinase*: (CPK) *or Creatine Kinase* (CK):** This enzyme is found in heart muscle, skeletal muscle and brain tissue. There are three isoenzymes of CPK known as CPK-MM found in skeletal muscle, CPK-BB in brain tissue and CPK-MB in heart muscle. Measurement of these enzymes indicates the source of damage. Usually, CPK-MM isozyme is present in serum. CPK levels are increased in tissue damage conditions like falls, vigorous exercise, deep IM injection etc. Diagnosis of acute myocardial infarction is possible by measurement of CPK level.
16. ***Lactic acid Dehydrogenase*: (LDH or LD):** This enzyme interconverts lactate and pyruvate in the body and is present in all metabolising cells. There are five isoenzymes of LDH, namely LDH 1 to LDH 5, out of which the first two are present in the heart, third in the lungs, and fourth and fifth in the liver and skeletal muscles, respectively. Measurement of these enzymes points out where the damage is, and this helps in the diagnosis of myocardial infarction and liver and lung diseases.

    Other enzymes are discussed below under Liver Function Tests.

Liver Function Tests

The concentration of enzymes and other compounds in serum are measured in usual liver function tests. Specific functions of the liver cannot be quantified by these tests. However, they are useful in the diagnosis and watching the progress of liver diseases. Thus, bilirubin is a measure to indicate the overall liver function, whereas serum albumin level and Prothrombin time indicate the synthesis of protein in the liver. Similarly, alkaline phosphate estimation gives an idea about obstruction in bile flow, and the transaminase levels indicate liver injury or cell death.

***Albumin*:** It is a protein synthesised in the liver up to 10 to 15 g per day, of which 60% is found in ECF and the balance 40% in the serum.

If there are fewer albumins in the serum, oedema may occur. As there is less protein (albumin) in the blood, less amount of drugs can be bound to it, and hence there is a significant increase in free drug concentration in the blood. If it is not eliminated quickly, as in kidney damage and other conditions, toxic effects of drugs may occur in the patient. Hypoalbuminemia is due to damaged kidneys, skin damage, as in burns, and increased catabolism due to many illnesses. Because of the short life of Albumin (20 days), it cannot confirm the change in liver function; however, it has some prognostic value. Albumin levels may increase rarely and after dehydration, shock or an individual's peculiar reactions. [Idiosyncratic].

***Bilirubin*:** It is tested to diagnose jaundice. If the serum bilirubin level is above 50 μ/mol/L, it indicates jaundice. In chronic liver diseases, an increased level of bilirubin is of prognostic value. Elevated levels of bilirubin may be due to increased production, decreased excretion, impaired transport, or a combination of these factors.

Enzymes

The following components and enzymes are measured in liver function tests:

1. Albumin	-	38.50 g/L
2. Bilirubin (total)	-	< 19 μ mol/L
3. Bilirubin (conjugated)	-	< 4 μ mol/L
4. Alanine Transaminase (ALT) or Serum Glutamate Pyruvate Transaminase (SGPT)	-	< 60 μ/lit
5. Aspartate Transaminase (AST) or Serum Glutamate Oxaloacetic Transaminase (SGOT)	-	< 35 μ /L
6. Alkaline Phosphatase (AP or ALP)	-	< 35 – 130 μ /L
7. γ-Glutamyl Transpeptidase	-	< 70 μ /L

Usually, enzyme concentration in healthy people is low; it is only when cells are damaged that their contents of them are released into the blood, and the levels are increased. Before analysing the blood for enzymes, one must understand the principles involved in the assay. The actual enzyme concentration is not measured in assays but only in the catalytic activity. Many enzymes are present in more than one tissue, and hence elevated levels of enzymes in blood may be due to damage to any one of the tissue. Apart from this, sample drawing time is also essential, as these enzymes may not be present immediately after tissue injury or vanish from the blood if the sample is drawn after a long time.

Alkaline Phosphatase

It is one of the important parameters checked in the Liver function test and discussed above.

Transaminases

There are two transaminases, aspartate transaminase (AST or SGOT) and alanine transaminase (ALT or SGPT). They are mainly found in hepatocytes and muscle cells, apart from some other tissues. AST levels are increased in liver diseases, myocardial infarction, surgery and injury, whereas ALT level is increased in viral and non-viral liver diseases. This is markedly increased in liver damage due to alcohol, paracetamol and viral infections.

γ Glutamyl Transpeptidase

It is present in more amounts in the liver, kidney and pancreas. It indicates hepatobiliary diseases. Hepatitis, cirrhosis, alcoholic liver disease, pancreatitis, and congestive heart failure increase this enzyme level.

Some drugs like phenytoin, phenobarbitone and rifampicin also increase this enzyme level. Apart from the above in liver function tests, the level of ammonia in blood and amylase in serum are also measured, if they are in excess, hepatic dysfunction and pancreatitis are indicated.

Renal Function Tests

Renal function tests are used to evaluate the kidney and its functions. The disease of the kidney can also be followed by testing nephron functions like glomerular filtration, blood flow and tubular transport.

Glomerular filtration is clinically tested by the tests like creatinine clearance, serum creatinine and serum urea. Renal plasma flow is tested by Para amino. 151ippurate (PAH). Similarly, tubular transport is tested by serum phosphate urate, urinary amino acids, maximal urinary osmolarity and acid bicarbonate loading.

Creatinine Clearance

Glomerular filtration rate (GFR) is estimated using creatinine clearance. The normal value for men is 140 to 240 L/day i.e., 70 $\pm$ 14 ml/min/sq.m and for women is 120 to 180 L/day i.e., 60 $\pm$ 10 ml/min/sq.m. Creatinine clearance is not useful to detect earlier stages of kidney damage because glomeruli is not damaged but just increase in size, hence only after 50% to 70% damage to glomerular filtration surface, a decrease in creatinine clearance is clearly detectable. Because of this problem serum creatinine is also measured along with creatinine clearance because creatinine production and excretion are constant if there is no kidney damage.

Serum Creatinine

If the GFR increases, serum creatinine concentration decreases and vice versa. Hence serum creatinine concentration is a useful index of GFR. It is increased only when there is kidney damage, however depends on some other factors like muscle mass, age etc. The maximum serum creatinine concentration in man with normal GFR is 1.2 mg/dl and in women 1 mg/dl. The formula for calculating creatinine clearance in men is as follows:

$$C_{L(creat)} = \frac{(140 - \text{Age in years})\ (\text{Body weight in Kg})}{72 \times (\text{Serum creatinine in mg / dL})}$$

For women the value should be multiplied by 0.85.

Usually if the GFR decreases by 50%, serum creatinine increases by 100%. For example, if the normal value of serum creatinine is 1.2 mg/dl with 50% reduction in renal function the value doubles to 2.4 mg/dl.

Serum Urea or Blood Urea Nitrogen (BUN)

Though the concentration of urea in blood depends on many factors like urine flow rate, production and metabolism of urea, a ratio between BUN and creatinine is useful to differentiate pre-renal, renal and post renal azotaemia. Azotaemia is a condition in which excess of nitrogenous waste products are retained in the blood.

If the ratio is more than 15, it indicates prerenal, post renal azotaemia. The increase in ratio may be due to uncontrolled diabetes, infections, and glucocorticoid therapy. Shock, dehydration and GI haemorrhage induce prerenal azotaemia. This ratio is less, in the cases of liver diseases, malnutrition, and in pregnancy.

Renal plasma flow: It is a difficult and costly test and not useful than GFR.

Renal concentration ability: It is a simple and helpful test. If there is less renal concentration ability it results in oedema and fibrosis.

Pulmonary Function Tests

There are many tests to check the pulmonary function like spirometry diffusing capacity, flow-volume loops etc. However, all are not essential to identify the deficiency in pulmonary function. There are two types of disorders of lungs one is restrictive disorder another one is obstructive disorder. The obstructive disorders are Chronic Obstructive Pulmonary Diseases (COPD), asthma, bronchitis and loss of lung's elastic recoil. In restrictive lung disorders due to increased diameter of airways during expiration, flow rates are increased.

Pulmonary Functions or Parameters

In order to understand the tests and their interpretation a clinical pharmacist must understand various pulmonary functions or parameters. They are -

1. ***Vital capacity* (VC):** It is the maximum volume of air that can be expired slowly and completely after a full respiratory effort.

2. ***Forced vital capacity*** **(FVC):** It is same as above (VC) but utilize a maximum forceful expiration.
3. ***Functional residual capacity*** **(FRC):** It is the volume of air in the lungs at the end of normal expiration when all respiratory muscles are relaxed. FRC has two components. Residual volume (RV) – the volume of air remaining in the lungs at the end of a maximal expiration and Expirator Reserve Volume (ERV) i.e., FRC = RV + ERV. The RV is normally accounts for about 25% of the TLC (Total Lung Capacity).
4. ***Forced Expirator Volume in* 1 *second*** **(FEV_1):** It is the volume of air force fully expelled during the first second after a full breath and normally comprises less than 75% of the vital capacity (VC).

Pulmonary Function Tests Including Spirometry

Pulmonary disorders can be evaluated usually by simple spirometry tests. It is one of the important tests and provides sufficient information. Using spirometry VC, FEV_1 and Peak Expiratory Flow (PEF) can be tested. The test procedure is easy to learn by both operator and patient and yields permanent, reproducible and accurate data. Spirometry test is useful to differentiate between obstruction and restrictive disorders and to estimate the severity of the disease.

Spirometry with determination of FVC, FEV_1 and Maximal Voluntary Ventilation (MVV) is performed in all patients with respiratory problems. Patients with larynx or trachea infection are tested by flow volume loop (FVL) test. Similarly, if weakness of respiratory muscle is suspected MVV, MIP, MEP and FVC (the lung mechanics) are carried out. If the clinical picture is not coinciding with results obtained by simple spirometry or when complete investigation of abnormal pulmonary process is required full testing may be done.

Interpretation of Pulmonary Function Tests

If the VC is less, even when there are normal flow rates, it indicates restrictive disease. Exponentially decreasing flows suggests Asthma. The severity of Asthma and the potential for response to bronchodilator can be adequately assessed by simple spirometry before and after inhalation of a bronchodilator aerosol. The response to treatment should be monitored by portable spirometry.

Retesting of pulmonary function after inhalation of a bronchodilator aerosol (e.g., Isoetharine) provides information about the reversibility of an obstructive process i.e., Asthma. Improvement in VC and/or FEV_1 of more than 15% is usually considered a bronchodilator response. Return of these parameters to normal following inhalation of bronchodilator aerosol indicates Asthma. Absence of a response to a single exposure to bronchodilator however does not preclude a beneficial response to maintenance therapy in patients with COPD.

Thyroid Function Tests

Introduction

Thyroid hormones are biosynthesized by iodinating the amino acid Tyrosine. For this biosynthesis iodine is collected and concentrated by thyroid gland from food and water we take. Tyrosine is iodinated either one or two sites and named monoiodothyrosine [MIT] or diiodothyrosine [DIT] respectively. One MIT and one DIT coupled to form Triiodothyronine [T3] or two molecules of DIT coupled to form Tetraiodothyronine [T4] the latter is otherwise known as Thyroxin. These T3 and T4 are embedded in a glycoprotein known as thyroglobulin as colloidal droplets in thyroid cells.

Later these thyroglobulin releases T3 and T4 in blood stream by the action of protease. Similar to drugs, these T3 and T4 also bind to proteins in the blood as Thyroxin binding globulin [TBG] [up to 80%] Thyroxin binding prealbumin [TBPA] and albumin [up to 20%]. Very less quantity of these [0.05 to 0.5%] is free in nature, not binding to any protein. The formation of T3 and T4 are influenced and controlled by a pituitary secreted hormone known as Thyroid Stimulating Hormone [TSH]. The physiological functions of thyroid hormone are to promote protein synthesis in all the body tissue and to increase oxygen consumption in liver, kidney, heart and skeletal muscles.

Tests for Thyroid Function

There are many tests available for testing how well thyroid gland is functioning. They are T3, T4, TSH and radioactive iodine up-take [RAIU] tests. Before the arrival of these modern tests, protein bound iodine [PBI] test was widely used which was less accurate and hence now a days not done. Thyroid scanning tests, Thyrotropin releasing hormone [TRH] test and T3 suppression tests are the other tests very rarely used for evaluating the function of thyroid gland. Hence the first four tests are described below.

1. ***T3 Tests:*** These tests are usually done to diagnose hyperthyroidism. Excess level of T3 [Triiodothyronine] will be present in patients who are hyperthyroid. However, this test is not useful to study hypothyroidism, because it shows abnormal only after the disease reaches severe stage. Also, during pregnancy and while using birth control pills, both T3 and 4 may show excess level due to the fact that estrogens present in these conditions, increase the proteins for binding. T3 also increases during the condition called Grave's disease which is an auto immune disorder. Hence usually TSH and free T4 tests are ordered together under these conditions.

Serum Total T3 is measured by Radio Immuno Assay. Obviously T3 level depends on the circulating proteins TBG, albumin etc. In order to overcome the problem of variation in TBG, T3 resin uptake tests are performed. This test reveals the unsaturated thyroid binding on TPG. Normally around 30% of TBG binding sites are occupied by thyroid hormone. By *in-vitro* analysis, ^{125}I T3 is added to patient's serum when a part of it binds to unoccupied TBG sites. If a resin is added to it after equilibration, it binds the remaining ^{125}I T3. The value obtained is reported as ratio or percentage of bound or unbound. In hypothyroidism, there are less occupied and more unoccupied TBG sites whereas opposite is the case with hyperthyroidism.

2. ***T4 Tests***: T4 is circulating in the blood either bound to protein or in unbound form as free molecules. Both these forms of T4 are measured in serum total T4 whereas only T4 is measured in Free T4 [FT4] or Free T4 Index [FT4I or FTI] tests. As already mentioned, level of protein present in blood alters these values. For example, in pregnancy and when using birth control tablets more protein binding sites are available for T4 to bind. Hence total T4 may be on the higher side but the patient need not be hyperthyroid as only the free T4 is physiologically active. Thus, hyperthyroid patients will have excess of FT4 or FTI value and if it is less, it indicates hypothyroidism. So, measuring FT4 or FTI is important. However low levels of T4 always not indicate hypothyroidism, because severe illness and prolong steroid use also reduces protein binding sites in blood and shows decreased level of T4.

   T4 is isolated by ion exchange column chromatography and determined by colorimetric method. FT4 is determined by a competitive protein binding method of analysis in which^{125}I T4 and serum are incubated and dialyzed to find out percentage of dialyzable ^{125}I T4. However, there may be some interference by the presence of inorganic iodides, mercuric compounds in T4 column chromatography method. Also, highly protein bound drugs affect the results of competitive protein binding method.

3. ***TSH Tests:*** It is done to measure the amount of Thyroid Stimulating Hormone present in the blood. Normally TSH is more when there is less amount of thyroxin secreted as in hypothyroidism and it is less or nil when excess of thyroxin is produced as in hyperthyroidism. Rarely there may be less amount of TSH, if the pituitary gland which secrets it, is affected. TSH is actually secreted as and when thyroxin level goes down in the blood and reduce or stop secreting when levels are excess, just like a thermostat switching on or off in an iron box or geyser. TSH is measured by Radio Immuno Assay [RIA].

4. ***Radioactive Iodine Uptake Test [RAIU]:*** It is a non-blood test in which patient is given a small amount of radioactive iodine and its uptake by

thyroid gland is determined. If excess of that is absorbed by the gland it indicates hyperthyroidism and less up, take indicate hypothyroidism. [Iodine is required for biosynthesis of T3 and T4 by thyroid gland]. This test has the disadvantage of cost, time, patient inconvenience and exposure to radiation. However, the above test is useful in T3 suppression tests and for calculating the dose when ^{131}I is used as a treatment modality as per Merck manual for medical practitioners.

The results of above Thyroid Function Tests are summarized in the following table:

Condition	T3	T4	TSH	RAIU
Hyperthyroidism	↑	↑	↓	↑
Hypothyroidism	↓	↓	↑	↓
Normal Value	85 - 185 ng/dl by RIA	5 - 11 µg/dl by RIA	0.4 - 4.8 µU/ml by RIA	At 5 hr =5 -15% At 24 hr =10 -35%

KEY: ↓ = Below normal ↑ = Above normal

Tests Associated with Cardiac Disorders

Patients may be affected by various cardiac disorders. The frequently encountered disorders are

(a) Angina pectoris
(b) Myocardial infarction
(c) Congestive cardiac failure
(d) Atherosclerosis.

There are many tests to diagnose, and estimates extend of damage due to these disorders. They help the clinician to take decision regarding medical or surgical management of patients.

***Types of tests*:** These tests are classified in to two categories, invasive and non-invasive tests. The non-invasive tests are

1. Auscultation
2. Blood tests
3. Chest x-ray
4. ECG
5. Echocardiography
6. MRI scans
7. Radio nuclide and
8. Stress tests.

The invasive test is cardiac catheterization [Angiography].

***Diagnosis of Cardiac Disorders*:** Diagnosis starts from collection of medication history of the patient and his/her family. It is followed by assessing risk factors and physical examination. Finally, patients are tested by few, or all the tests mentioned above, as one or two tests cannot diagnose the cardiac disorders with 100% accuracy. The detail of each of above test follows:

I. Non-Invasive Tests

1. ***Auscultation*:** This is nothing but testing the patient's heartbeat with stethoscope which helps to hear the normal and abnormal sounds of heartbeat. Changes in heartbeat associated with breathing and murmurs also heard with stethoscope. Variation in sound, rhythm, and murmur points to the fact that something is wrong with the heart and that is identified and confirmed by various tests mentioned below.

2. ***Blood Tests*:** The first test ordered after physical examination of the patient with stethoscope is blood tests. Number of components of blood is measured and they give valuable hints about impending or ongoing cardiac disorder. These tests and their normal values and risk values are given in the following table.

Blood Tests Value

Tests	Normal Value	Risk Value
Total cholesterol	< 200 mg/dl	> 240 mg/dl
LDL	< 100 mg/dl	> 160 mg/dl
HDL	> 60 mg/dl	< 40 mg/dl
Triglycerides	< 150 mg/dl	> 200 mg/dl
Fibrinogen	< 300 mg/dl	> 460 mg/dl
Lipoprotein [a]	< 14 mg/dl	> 19 mg/dl

Apart from the above electrolytes in blood are also measured which is described elsewhere in this book. Arterial blood gas determination also helps in diagnosis and treatment of patients with shock and myocardial infraction [MI]. Oxygen level and acid-base balances are also tested.

3. ***Chest X-Ray*:** A chest x-ray gives the pictures of internal organs like, heart, lungs and chest wall. It can reveal the signs of heart failure, enlarged heart and edema. Usually frontal and lateral chest views are filmed to detect heart diseases by evaluating heart size, heart shape and the lungs.

4. ***Electrocardiogram*:** It records the electrical activity and rhythm of the heart. It is recorded normally by 12 lead electrodes from the skin surface in three planes, anterior, posterior and lateral. The electrical signal of each heart beat is recorded by the ECG machine. Slow heart rate [Bradycardia] and fast heart rate [Tachycardia] produces rhythm

abnormalities which can be visualized by ECG. But we must remember an abnormal reading does not always indicate a problem with heart, similar to normal reading does not rule out heart problems. Hence ECG is combined with stress tests, that is, ECG is recorded while the patient is undergoing stress tests on a tread mill or exercise bike.

5. ***Echocardiography* [ECHO]:** It produces a moving picture of heart using sound waves that provides information about the structure [size and shape] and pumping function of the heart. It also reveals the movement of heart valves and heart muscle thickness. After applying a lubricating gel over the chest, a hand-held device called transducer is passed over it, so that there is continuous contact between the transducer and skin. The images produced can show the damages to heart muscle due to poor blood supply and non-functional area of heart. Thus, echocardiography is the method of choice for diagnosing abnormalities of heart at birth, valve dysfunction etc.

   Echo tests are carried out by more than one method. M.mode echo cardiography, Two-dimensional echo, Doppler echo and Contrast echo are often used methods to diagnose cardiac disorders. M.mode echo use pulsed-reflected ultra sound to look at the internal cardiac structures. Two-dimensional [2D] echo produce spatially correct images of the heart and can be recorded as video images. Doppler echo is the method of recording the flow of blood in around the heart using ultrasound. Contrast echo is nothing but M.mode and 2 D tests only, the difference being they are conducted after injecting contrast medium into cardio vascular circulation.

6. ***MRI scan*:** Magnetic Resonance Imaging [MRI] produces detailed pictures of heart. Patients are scanned using magnetic and radio waves when lying inside a tunnel like scanner. The computer attached to the scanner creates the picture – both still and moving – of the heart and major blood vessels. The disadvantages of MRI scan are it is expensive and images are formed slowly. It cannot be used on patients with metallic prostheses or implants. However, it is safer than CT scan, because it does not use ionizing radiation for image formation. It is a valuable tool in diagnosing cardiomyopathies, myocarditis, myocardial ischemia, iron overload, congenital heart diseases and vascular diseases.

   MRI uses a strong and uniform magnetic field. Its field strength is measured by a unit called 'Tesla' [T]. Usual MRI machines are of 1.5 T, but other machines with 0.2 to 7 T are also available. A special type of MRI for using in specifically in cardiac disorders is used now-a-day. It is known as cardio vascular Magnetic Resonance Imaging [CMR] or cardiac MRI. Here basic MRI is optimized, so that they use ECG gating and rapid imaging techniques or sequences. In this CMR a sequence called spin echo is used in which the blood appears block in colour so that a contrasting agent need not be used.

7. ***Radio nuclide test*:** Here a small amount of radio active substance [an isotope] is injected into the blood of the patient. A camera is held near the chest which picks up the radiation released by the isotope as it passes through the heart, indicating the areas where there is poor blood supply. Thus, they provide more detailed information than the Stress ECG test described below. From the collected information Clinician can assess how strongly the heart pumps and the blood flow to muscular walls of heart.

8. ***Stress tests*:** These tests are carried out using a tread mill and/or exercise bike. During this test the heart of the patient work hard and beat faster. An ECG may be connected to the patient so as to record the cardiac activity. If the patient cannot exercise, he or she may be given drugs to increase the heart rate. If the patient' coronary arteries are deposited with plague and thus narrowed it cannot supply enough blood with oxygen to meet the increased need during these stress tests. Hence the following signs and symptoms can be detected:

   (a) Breathing Difficulty
   (b) Chest Pain
   (c) Abnormal heart rate or blood pressure and
   (d) Abnormal changes in heart rhythm and electrical activity which are measured using ECG and other equipment.

   During stress tests pictures of heart are taken and that is compared with pictures of heart taken while the patient is at rest. They give an indication of heart's functions.

II. Invasive Tests

1. ***Cardiac Catheterization or Coronary Angiography:*** It is a technique in which a thin, flexible catheter is passed along vein or artery into the heart and connected vessels either for diagnosis or treatment of cardiac disorders. The catheter is put into the blood vessel in arm or upper thigh or neck. It is then threaded into the coronary artery with the help of x-ray images. A dye is injected through the catheter to visualize the arteries supplying blood to the heart. All these procedures are done under local anesthesia.

   Then numbers of x-ray pictures are taken which indicate any block in the arteries. However, this test cannot detect blockages in micro vascular diseases because they usually do not cause any blockage in large coronary arteries. Nevertheless, cardiac catheterization or coronary angiography is relatively safe procedure and serious complications are rare. Possible problems, 1 or 2 in 1000, are cardiac arrhythmias and ventricular fibrillation. If angina develops during the test, it is treated with sublingual nitroglycerin tablets.

During catheterization, intra cardiac pressure, blood gas saturation and pressure pulse tracings can also be measured. B.P can be measured at various points of heart by which pressure gradient across the valves can be calculated. Cardiac output and vascular resistance are also calculated which are useful quantitative information for further procedures. These tests are avoided in patients with severe infections or brain damage. Nausea, vomiting, cough, sense of warmth are the side effects of these tests.

Questions

Short Answer Questions

1. Write a note on significance of lab tests.
2. How are lab tests interpreted?
3. Write a note on Biochemical data.
4. What happen when electrolytes balance is disturbed?
5. Write the role of drugs in disturbing electrolytes balance with examples.
6. Write a note on biosynthesis of Thyroid hormone.
7. What are T3, T4, and TSH? Write few lines about each.
8. Write a note on an invasive test for cardiac disorder.

Long Answer Questions

9. What are haematological tests? Explain important tests and the range.
10. What is the significance of Liver function tests? Explain how they are carried out.
11. Write short notes on: A] Renal function tests B] Pulmonary function tests
12. Discuss the importance and methods of tests for electrolytes.
13. Explain various Thyroid function tests.
14. Enumerate the tests associated with cardiac disorder.

CHAPTER 14

DRUG INFORMATION CENTER

Introduction

Traditionally, pharmacists used to give just the needed information like dosage, use and storage of the drugs to the patients visiting hospitals and retail outlets. This traditional role has changed now from product-oriented to patient oriented. He is now expected to provide all information about drugs and also other related information like availability, substitute, ADR, Research findings etc. Hence drug information centres are established in all the big hospitals and other places. As the custodian of the knowledge bank (Drug Information Center, DIC), Pharmacist is expected to play a much larger role as teachers and information provider.

Need for Drug Information Centers

Due to fast scientific developments and consequent research possibilities in the last few decades lot of new drugs and formulations are added daily to the book of drugs throughout the world. Now the volume of information available about drugs is impossible to manage or remember by an individual, however, experienced or educated he may be. Hence some sort of arrangement is needed to collect, edit and arrange such a huge quantity of information. Thus drug information centres have become an essential entity.

Moreover, all the informations published are not needed to everybody. For example, for a cancer hospital, information related to its activities are essential, whereas other information are only of academic interest. Hence someone is needed to collect and edit the needed information and bring it to their attention. This itself is a tremendous task as there are few journals and magazines in each sub-division of science nowadays. As the information technology revolution has resulted in the flooding of information from every nook and corner of the world, the need for someone or service to sort out those information is felt. Hence Drug Information services become necessary.

A busy practising physician or surgeon is in need of some information urgently in a complicated situation. He has to put in a lot of effort, wasting his precious time and energy to collect such information. If a centre or service is available for ready reference, it will be of great help to him. Moreover, even the general public can clarify their doubts regarding the drugs they use or diseases they have, by enquiring with Drug Information centres, without much effort or money. If such a centre is not available, they have to disturb or depend only on the treating physician, for which they are reluctant and hence deprived of even essential information, resulting in complications.

Thus the need for Drug Information Center is evident.

Sources of Information

Based on the origin and nature of the information, the sources of information can be divided into three. They are:

1. Primary sources
2. Secondary sources and
3. Tertiary sources

1. ***Primary Sources***: These are the original informations generated by research scholars and scientists and published either in scientific journals and/or presented in conferences, seminars etc. These information are not condensed, interpreted or edited by a second party. Other examples are patent applications, theses, dissertations and technical reports.
2. ***Secondary Sources***: These information are collected from all or any one of the above primary sources and edited or interpreted by others other than the original authors. Usually, it is done for a specific purpose or audience. Examples are, review articles, handbooks, textbooks, encyclopedias and computerised services like abstracting or indexing services, which are described below.
3. ***Tertiary Sources***: The information derived from both or either of the above sources is known as Tertiary information. Here the information provided is composite and in a diluted version. Examples are guides, literature and pamphlets issued by manufacturers etc. Information gathered from people who attended the conferences and seminars are also falling under this category.

   It is clear from the above primary sources of information are reliable, accurate and most current in nature. On the other hand, secondary and tertiary information is less accurate or less recent in nature because they have passed through several authors or publishers.

Computerised Services

This is one of the secondary sources of information, where details are collected from various sources, edited and published as databases in CD.ROM format or uploaded in websites or portals of the internet. They are further differentiated into indexing services and abstracting services. Both these services are very much useful for libraries and information centres like Drug Information centres, where online searching can be used to search the database of remote locations without networking facilities and for use by single users, on the other hand, CD is used when many people use the same computer.

Abstracting Services: As the name indicates, it contains the summaries or abstracts of original reports. It also interprets the original report according to editorial guidelines. Popular examples are

(a) Drugdex
(b) International Pharmaceutical Abstract
(c) Pharmline.

Pharmline database (http://www.pharmline.com) is an abstracting system that deals with drugs and professional pharmacy practice. This database abstracts articles on pharmacy practice and clinical use of drugs from over 100 English pharmacy and medical journals and is produced by National Health Service Information specialists.

International pharmaceutical abstracts is produced by American Society of Health System (ASHP) pharmacists. It has abstracted from the articles published in more than 750 pharma, medical and other health-related journals published worldwide. This service has been there since 1970. It is a paid service, available via http://www.ashp.org/ipal.

***Indexing Services*:** Examples of indexing services are:

1. Medline
2. BIOSIS [Biosciences information service] previews
3. Clinalert
4. Embase
5. IDIS (Iowa drug Information System)

An indexing service is not interpreting the original article but provides only the indexed topic and the original abstract or full text.

1. ***Medline*:** Medical, dental and nursing journals are indexed here, which was prepared by the US National Library of Medicine from 1966 onwards, some 11 million records from more than 4300 journals are indexed in this service. Important pharmacy journals like "The Pharmaceutical Journal" is not covered. This database is updated daily, and CD versions like OVID and silver platter are also available.

Medline systems via the internet include 'Pubmed' and 'Biomed net'. They just differ in their presentation and search systems.

2. ***BIOSIS***: [Biosciences information service] It gives the journal, meetings, books, and patents data we need to prepare research projects, grant proposals and follow trends in the life sciences. BIOSIS research databases provide us with today's most current sources of life sciences information, including journals, conferences, patents, books, review articles and more
3. ***Clinalert***: It provides pharmacists, physicians and other healthcare professionals with comprehensive summaries of adverse drug reactions, drug interactions and market withdrawals from over 100 key medical and research journals from around the world
4. ***Embase***: It is produced by Elsevier science. It is a major database covering pharmaceutical and biomedical journals. More than 4000 international journals are indexed, and about 8 million records from 1974 are available.
5. ***Iowa Drug Information Service (IDIS)***: It is produced by the University of Iowa, USA. It covers about 200 important English medical and pharmaceutical journals. Only the articles relating to the treatment of humans are indexed, and they are available in their full versions. It is available both in the Internet and as CD ROM.

Advantages and Disadvantages

The advantages of Information resources are,

(a) They present the information in a nutshell and are catalogued in many ways, like author-wise, subject-wise, and year of publication wise and hence it is easy to retrieve the needed information in a fraction of a minute.

(b) The computerised information sources are, in particular, offering the information seeker the wide possibilities of going through worldwide literatures, which is impossible for a research scholar if searched manually.

(c) This information is available on the internet to a certain extent so that anybody, at any time, in any place, gets the information even in his hand-held device as sometimes such information may be required urgently, for example, for a doctor treating critical emergency cases.

The disadvantages of drug information sources are few.

(a) Unless this information is updated then and there, we end up in getting old or known information which may not be helpful.

(b) The collection of information available in databases is costlier, running to lakhs of rupees or can get after paying a huge yearly subscription.

(c) As mentioned above, secondary and tertiary sources of information are edited by third parties and serve little or specific purposes.

Retrieval of Information

As the database contains millions and millions of pieces of informations, retrieval of information requires some skill. If you are able to search with precious or correct terms, the retrieval is easier. To do that, the indexing language of the database (controlled vocabulary or thesaurus or keywords) should be used. All possible synonyms, if used, make the search easier, on the other hand, if a common language or free text is used, all relevant information may not be obtained. Hence before starting the search, a straightforward question must be framed. For example, "How effective are ACE inhibitors in the treatment of heart failure?".

The next step is to choose relevant subject headings or keywords to include in the search. These can be included in the search question using the Boolean operators (and/or/not) to get relevant citations. Some databases, like Medline and Embase, use subheadings like Adverse effects, Use, Diagnosis etc., to direct the search towards the specific question.

Systematic Approach in Answering Drug Information Queries

Drug information queries cannot be answered casually, just like that in any customer care Centre or public relations office, as it involves lifesaving drugs. In order to give correct, vital and needed information, the drug information Centre pharmacist has to approach it in a systematic manner. Watanabe and Conner have described well such an approach for answering DI queries in their paper 'Principles of Drug Information services' [Drug Intell Publ, Hamilton IL: 15,1978]. Incorporating those suggestions, before answering the question DIC pharmacist should ask the following counter questions either to the enquirer or himself and then answer. The questions are,

1. Who is enquiring?
2. What is his purpose?
3. What is the background information?
4. What category the query belongs to?
5. How to retrieve the answer quickly?
6. Is the answer retrieved worth disseminating?
7. How best the answer can be provided? and
8. What is the feedback?

Summary of Services of Drug Information Center

1. Establishing and maintaining a system for getting information about drugs.
2. Providing information to Inservice training or continuous education programmes.
3. Answering queries from Research scholars, PG students, Poison information centre etc.
4. Answering questions from physicians regarding drugs and therapy.
5. Preparation and distribution of periodical Drug Information bulletins to doctors, nurses, pharmacists and students of these courses.
6. Helping in the preparation and maintenance of the Hospital Formulary or Drugs list.
7. Critical analysis of pharmacy literature and filing them with comments and opinions.
8. Above all, clearing the doubts and answering the enquiries of the general public regarding their treatment.
9. Producing educational materials for Mass Education Programs.
10. Coordinating with outside agencies relating to Drug information, in serving the community at large and
11. Maintaining a record of all enquiries.

Questions

Short Answer Questions

1. Write briefly about the need for Drug Information Center.
2. What are the sources of Drug Information?
3. List the function of the Drug Information Centre.
4. How will you answer a drug information query?

Long Answer Questions

5. Write in detail about the secondary source of information, including computerised sources.
6. List the advantages and disadvantages of information resources.

CHAPTER 15

POISON INFORMATION CENTRE

Introduction

Virtually all materials are used to poison living things. It ranges from high doses of comparatively harmless drugs to cosmetics like nail polish, shaving lotion, etc.

Hence, poison is defined as any substance that, when consumed in any form, causes a toxic effect on the body. The scientific study of poisons is known as Toxicology.

Identification of poison in poison cases is very difficult. Hence in poison cases, only the patient has to be treated, not the poison. That is to say, while treating, measure and monitor all vital parameters of the patient and his symptoms and treat accordingly.

Clinical Manifestations

Poisoning may be acute or chronic. In acute poisoning, the effect of the poison is immediate and severe. If not treated quickly, death may result. The symptoms are vomiting, diarrhoea, convulsions, unconsciousness and coma. The poison may be detected in vomiting, stool or urine. In the case of chronic poisoning, the effect may be relatively slow, gradual, less severe and for a long period. Environment or habits may be the reason for this type of poisoning, hence, if removed or stopped, the causes and symptoms disappear. The symptoms are chronic ill health, repeated GI Irritation or disturbances, weakness etc.

Types of Poisons

Poisons can be classified according to their origin or mechanism of action. Synthetic poison or natural poison is the major division in the classification according to the origin, and natural poison may be of vegetable, animal or mineral origin.

Depending on the mechanism of action, poisons can be classified as follows:

(a) ***Irritants*:** They may be of inorganic, organic or mechanical irritants. Inorganic substances are either metallic or non-metallic. Phosphorous, Chloride, Iodine, and Bromine are the examples of non-metallic poisons; lead, mercury, copper etc., are the metallic poisons. Organic poisons are either of animal origin, like venoms of snakes, scorpions and insects, or of vegetable origin, like Ergot, Aloe, Capsicum, and Castor seeds. Sometimes powdered glass or diamond is used as poison which is an example of a mechanical irritant.

(b) ***Corrosive Poisons*:** Strong acids and alkalis are examples of corrosive poisons. They destroy the internal organs, especially the GI tract, when taken orally by their strong corrosive property. Hydrochloric acid, sulphuric acid, and sodium hydroxide are usually misused to kill self or others.

(c) ***Neurotic Poisons*:** They act on the central nervous system and cause toxic effects. They may act on Brain, Spinal cord or on peripheral nerves. Sedatives, hypnotics, insecticides and cocaine are an example of brain poisons, Nux vomica act on the spine and curare alkaloids act on the peripheral nerves.

(d) ***Cardiac Poisons*:** Digitalis, Strophanthus, and Aconite are examples of cardiac poisons.

(e) ***Respiratory Depressants*:** Poisonous gases like carbon monoxide and coal gas depress respiratory organs, and the patient dies due to poor oxygen supply.

(f) ***Other Poisons*:** Drugs like analgesics, antipyretics, antihistamines and antidepressants, if consumed in higher doses, produce many toxic effects and finally results in the death of the patient.

Antidotes

If the poison is identified with certainty, specific treatments with specific measures like the use of antidotes can be undertaken.

For example, if a narcotic agent poison is confirmed, intravenous naloxone dilates the constricted pupil. Similarly, IV Flumazenil produces arousal in benzodiazepine poison cases. Thus, specific antidotes help in the quick neutralisation of poisons.

There are four types of antidotes; physical antidote, chemical antidote, physiological antidote and universal antidote.

Physical Antidotes

Inert, harmless substances are administrated to poison cases just to physically absorb the poison and then to eliminate it from the body. They do not react with any poison to neutralise them. Sometimes absorption of poison is inhibited or delayed using substances like egg albumin, fat or oil. Banana is given to absorb and bind the glass pieces. Activated charcoal is used to absorb alkaloidal poisons; care should be taken not to administer oil or fat to phosphorous poison cases because they are soluble in it.

Chemical Antidotes

These are chemical substances which react and neutralise the chemical poisons. They form nontoxic products as precipitates or soluble compounds inside the body. For instance, acids are neutralised with magnesium oxide or calcium oxide, lead is precipitated with potassium sulphate or sodium sulphate. Other examples are the administration of tannins to alkaloid poison cases and lime water to oxalic acid poison.

Physiological Antidotes

Substances which act against poison and produce just the opposite effects are used to counteract toxic effects. They are called antagonists. Up to which extent they counteract the poison and effects produced by antagonists themselves are the point of concern. Examples are given below separately.

Universal Antidotes

If the identity of the poison is not known with certainty, the universal antidote is used. They neutralise the acids, absorb alkaloidal poisons and chelate metals etc. The composition of universal antidotes is as follows:

Magnesium – 1 part
Activated charcoal – 2 parts
Tannic acid – 1 part

It is administered at a dose of 20 to 30 gm in 200 ml of water and given once or twice only. *Various poisons and specific Antidotes with doses are given below:*

Poison	Antidote	Dose
Iron Salts	Deferoxamine	15 mg/kg/hr
Lead	Calcium EDTA	50 to 75 mg/kg/day IM or IV in divided doses for a maximum of 5 days
Arsenic, Gold and Mercury	BAL. (Dimercaprol)	3 to 5 mg/kg/4 hourly IM for 2 days followed by 2 5 mg to 3 mg/kg/6 hourly for 7 days

Table *Contd...*

Poison	Antidote	Dose
	Penicillamine	1 gm orally daily 4 divided doses before meals.
Narcotic drugs like Morphine	Naloxone	1 to 2 mg or more IM or IV or SC.
Barbiturates	Coramine	Coramine IV at a dose of 5 ml increased to 10 ml in 15 minutes followed by 20 ml every 30 minutes till reflexes return.
Paracetamol	Acetyl cysteine	Loading dose 140 mg/kg. Then 70 mg/kg orally every 4 hours until serum level of paracetamol is zero
Cardio tonic drugs like Tricyclic antidepressants Quinidine etc	Sodium bicarbonate	1 to 2 mg/kg. Care should be taken as antidote may produce heart failure.
Physostigmine	Atropine	Test dose of 1 to 2 mg until symptoms of atropinism like Tachycardia, dilated pupil appear. Repeat the dose every 10 to 15 minutes until secretions stop.
Organo phosphorous compounds like Insecticides	Atropine followed by Parlidoxime	After cholinergic symptoms are controlled by atropine, parlidoxime can be given in doses of 1 gm IV. Repeat every 3 to 4 hours if necessary or give 250 to 400 mg/hour by infusion
Thallium	Prussian blue	--

Poison Information Centre [PIC]

Importance of PIC

Poisoning can be intentional or accidental and occur at any time. Obviously, if not treated immediately, it may be fatal. Hence there is always urgency in providing needed information. Almost all enquiries are by phone, and the reply must be given then and there at once. As it is a matter of life and death Poison Information Centres must be open round the clock for all 24 hours and all the days of the year without any holiday. Thus, it differs from Drug Information Centre, where the enquiries are not always urgent except for rare occasions.

Sources of Poison

There are many sources of poison, ranging from natural sources to synthetic sources. Natural sources include plants, animals or minerals, whereas synthetic sources are cosmetics, household items and pharmaceuticals.

Most of the time, chemicals, including drugs, are used as a poison. Chemicals usually available for a common man are from agricultural or horticultural sources. Rarely do laboratory chemicals cause poison. Next source of poison common to the majority of the Indian population is poisonous plants of wild growth. Fungi, cosmetics and household items like disinfectants, acids or even diamonds are used to commit suicide. Children accidentally swallow anything that comes to their hands. Thus, the sources of poison are vast and unimaginable.

Information about Poisons

In order to treat the poison cases effectively and immediately, all the information about the poison must be available. Hence the data should be collected beforehand and kept ready. But in practice, there are a number of problems in treating poison cases. Most of the time, what substances caused the poisoning is not known because the patient may not be in a position to reveal it. The persons accompanying or admitting the patients must bring the container, box, tube or paper found near the patient to the treating hospital, from which many times poisons can be identified. Next important problem is the quantity or dose of poison consumed by the patient, which has to be just guessed.

The third problem is the composition of the product consumed. For drugs and formulations, they are completely declared on labels, whereas, for other industrial products, it is not known. Hence that, information for at least commonly used poisons should be collected from manufacturers, and antidotes found and kept ready to use them in emergency situations. Even after this, some problems, like converting raw material to the finished product and its nature, are not known, as only the raw material used is revealed by the manufacturer. Sometimes manufacturers are reluctant to disclose their secret formula, but when compelled by law for the purpose of treating poisons, they reveal it, and that should be kept confidential. In a few instances, manufacturers change the composition without declaring it on labels. Thus, treatment of poison cases is very difficult, and most of the time, only symptomatic treatment is given.

However, a poison information centre should collect poison information as much as possible from as many sources as well. Usually, reference books available are,

1. Chemical toxicology of commercial products – By Glason *et al.*
2. Treatment of common acute poisoning – clinical – By Mathew. H. *et al.*
3. Hand Book of poisoning – By Driesbach
4. Extra pharmacopoeia
5. Merck Index etc.

Storage of Information

Information collected as above should be arranged in such a way that it should be retrieved as quickly as possible. In the olden days, they were arranged alphabetically in written cards and handled manually. Nowadays, the computer stores and retrieves information in a fraction of a second.

In order to have as much information as possible about each poison, the following format can be followed.

1. Name of the poison
2. Synonym
3. Source: Synthetic / plant/animal / mineral
4. Family (In case of plant or animal poison)
5. Description of external characters (macroscopy)
6. Habitat
7. Minimum lethal dose
8. Toxic effects
9. Symptoms
10. Pharmacokinetic properties
11. Treatment including antidotes
12. Supportive therapy
13. Prognosis
14. Any other relevant points and
15. References

Service by PIC -- Providing Information

It is not just mechanical work to be carried out by any non-healthcare professional. It requires expertise in providing needed information with all professional details in the shortest time possible. For this, one needs to have an understanding of the basic principles of poison treatment. That is why a brief outline of treatment of poison cases is given below (The purpose ends with that, at the maximum, a pharmacist can give first aid to such cases and should not attempt to give treatment to poison cases)

Depending upon the time and whether first aid has been given to the patient or not, the information to be given varies. Hence that should be enquired first, for that, the detail about the person enquiring must be asked. Professional or clinical information is required for doctors, nurses and other health care professionals, but the general public needs to know what is the first aid and what to do next. Advise them accordingly and instruct them to contact you later after taking the patient to a nearby hospital or clinic. More information, if required, can be provided during the second call.

As far as possible, detailed information should be given directly to the doctor, not to a third party. All these conversations depend on the pharmacist's discretion and skill. Details of each enquiry should be properly recorded in registers.

***Follow up*:** The job of the pharmacist of the Drug Information Centre is not over with providing information on the poison cases. He has to follow it up, and relevant details obtained from the treating physician, nurses, or relatives of the patient should also be recorded. These details may be useful for future cases and appreciated by physicians.

General Treatment of Poison Cases

It is obvious that poison cases should be treated as early as possible, otherwise, poisons get absorbed into the systems and start damaging vital organs one by one, and finally, the patient collapses.

It is better to identify the poison before the treatment is started. However, in the majority of the cases, it is not possible to identify the poison; hence the plasma analysis has to be carried out without delay, which may require time to reveal the result. The treating physician need not wait till the result of the analysis; he can start the following general treatment at once:

1. Removal of unabsorbed poison from the body to prevent further absorption.
2. Excretion of absorbed poison.
3. Treating general symptoms of the patient and
4. Maintaining the patient's general condition.

After identifying the poison, specific treatment can be started with specific antidotes. However, the above line of general treatment need not be stopped.

1. Removal of Unabsorbed Poison

Poison might have gone through various routes of the body. Depending on the route, various measures should be adopted to remove the poison from the body. If it is an inhalant poison through the nose, first of all, the patient should be taken to fresh air for respiration, followed by artificial respiration in hospitals. Poisons entered through skin, eyes, or wounds can be removed by washing them with plain, warm water. If a specific antidote is available, they are used to neutralise the poison. Sometimes poisons like venoms of snakes, scorpions, insects etc., are administered by them by sting or injection; such poisons are removed by making incisions at the site of the bite, and contaminated blood is drained out. More blood with poison can be removed by suction.

Poison by the oral route is a very common method of poisoning. It is removed by following methods:

1. Inducing vomiting by giving Ipecac or Apomorphine.
2. Stomach washing or Gastric Lavage by forcefully administering much water through the mouth of the patient, which dilutes the poison and induces vomiting.
3. *Purgation or Catharsis*: If considerable time is passed after oral ingestion of the poison, purgation should also be induced with strong cathartics, like Sorbitol, Magnesium sulphate or Sodium sulphate
4. Inert substances like activated charcoal are given orally at a dose of 50 gm in 300 ml of water to adsorb the poison. The dose should be repeated every 4th hour.

2. Excretion of Absorbed Poison

If considerable time, say about 6 hours, is elapsed after poisoning, poison might have entered the intestine and been absorbed in considerable amounts. Hence, inducing vomiting or stomach washing is not useful. The following methods of excreting absorbed poison can be tried.

(a) Use of Diuretics: Chlorothiazide and/or mannitol are administered intravenously to eliminate the poison through urine.

(b) Cathartics: Strong cathartics are used to induce purgation.

(c) Hot bags are used to increase sweating.

(d) Haemodialysis is used to eliminate some poisons like salicylates, barbiturates, thiocyanates and bromides. Peritoneal dialysis is done on children if salicylate poison is diagnosed.

3. Treating General Symptoms of the Patient

When the poison is not identified, the only option available is treating the patient according to symptoms. For example, if too much pain is there, morphine is given, if circulating failure is expected, cardiac stimulants are used, similarly, for respiratory problems, artificial respiration is given. Patients showing symptoms of dehydration are treated with electrolyte infusions.

4. Maintaining Patient's General Health Conditions

Along with treatment for poisoning, general therapy is given to maintain or improve the patient's general condition. To prevent upper respiratory tract infections in unconscious patients, prophylactic antibiotics are given. Hypotension and hypothermia (low body temp) are taken care of. Thus, intensive supportive therapy is essential to save the patient. Acid-base balance, low sugar, low potassium etc., are monitored in the blood plasma, and suitable corrective actions are taken.

Questions

Short Answer Questions

1. Write briefly about the importance of PIC.
2. What are the sources of Poison?
3. Classify poisons.
4. Write a note on antidotes.

Long Answer Questions

5. Explain how information about poison is provided in a poison information centre.
6. Write an essay about the general treatment of poison cases.
7. What are antidotes? Classify and give examples.

CHAPTER 16

PHARMACOVIGILANCE

Definition

W.H.O. defines Pharmacovigilance as the science and activities relating to the detection, assessment, understanding and prevention of adverse effects or any other possible medicine-related problems.

Need for Pharmacovigilance

It is a known fact that almost all drugs can cause harm if misused or abused. But some drugs produce adverse effects even at a normal dose that baffled the health care team. In order to find out those adverse effects and the reason for them, everybody involved in the treatment of the patient needs to be vigilant, analytical and careful. Thus, the need for monitoring drug treatment was felt, and it was redoubled after the 'Thalidomide' tragedy of the 1960s.

Though the process of introducing new drugs was tightened and lengthened after1960s [see chapter on clinical pharmacy], it cannot be delayed indefinitely. A new drug cannot be tested on crores of people in a clinical research laboratory. That is possible only after the drug is marketed in various countries with varying populations differing in race, ethnicity, environment, customs and habits. The results of the use of the new drug in risky people like, children, old people and pregnant women also has to be gathered as clinical trials are not done on these people normally. Hence 'Post Marketing Surveillance' [PMS] is the only option available before the drug regulators of the world to detect ADR and other problems. As this surveillance has to be carried out for many years after the marketing of the drug, there arises a need for a program to monitor, collect and document information about ADR pouring in periodically. Also, the information is from different countries and with a long time gap in between, and hence an international agency to do that work was felt by health care professionals. Thus W.H.O. started the Pharmacovigilance program by realising its need and importance. It is now functioning through National Pharmacovigilance Centers in member countries which are all coordinated by two WHO centres, one at Uppsala, the WHO collaborating centre for international drug monitoring, and another pharmacovigilance department of WHO in Geneva.

Aims of Pharmacovigilance

The primary aims of the Pharmacovigilance program are,

1. To improve patient care and safety
2. To enhance public health
3. To encourage monitoring understanding and training in pharmacovigilance programs, thereby alerting health care team and the general public and
4. To evaluate drug's benefits, risks and effectiveness and thereby to promote the safe and rational use of drugs.

In order to achieve the above aims Pharmacovigilance program has to be broad-based, and its scope should not be restricted or narrower. It has to include all the stakeholders of drug use in this program.

Scope of Pharmacovigilance

The scope of pharmacovigilance has been widened to include herbal, traditional and complementary medicines, blood products, biological, medical devices and vaccines. According to WHO, many other issues are also of relevance to the science of pharmacovigilance. They are substandard medicines, medication errors, lack of efficacy, use of medicines for indications that are not approved and for which there is an inadequate scientific basis, case reports of acute and chronic poisoning, assessment of medicine-related mortality, abuse and misuse of medicines, and adverse interactions of medicines with chemicals, other medicines and foods and drinks.

This, apart from the scope of pharmacovigilance, also extends from an individual patient to the Government to the entire society. However, let us restrict its application to some important areas so as to understand its significance and opportunities to work with.

1. ***Pharmacovigilance and clinical pharmacy practice*:** Therapeutic Drug Monitoring [TDM] and Drug Therapy Review are the important tools in the pharmacovigilance program of clinical practice. It has a great impact on the quality of health care. The information gathered during this program, if relevant, has to be conveyed to all healthcare providers, other pharmacovigilance centres and health policy developers. Thus, an effective patient care can be ensured.
2. ***Pharmacovigilance and medicine policy*:** In order to frame a national drug policy, a pharmacovigilance program is of much use to the

authorities, as it provides needed information about which drugs are not suitable in community settings and which other drugs can be promoted in national health programs etc. through such policies the government can forge links between various partners of pharmacovigilance program such as pharmaceutical industries, universities of health sciences, voluntary social organisations and professional associations who in turn promote the rational and safe use of drugs.

3. ***Pharmacovigilance and drugs control*:** The pharmacovigilance program is more helpful to Drugs control department than others as it makes their work easier. Drugs control organisations are gathering information about spurious drugs, sub-standard drugs, etc., through their own vigilance and intelligence wings. The pharmacovigilance centres, by monitoring drug therapy, provide much-needed information about the drug's quality, side effects etc., to them. Based on this information and input, the drugs regulatory department can start their investigation and weed out any problem drug from the market.

   Pharmacovigilance programs also emphasise monitoring of clinical trials, medicines of alternative systems and vaccines. Thus, it opens a link between all parties who have an interest in medicine safety and ensures that they all function in coordination with each other.

4. ***Pharmacovigilance and public health program*:** Many developing countries are implementing at least a few public health programs at the same time. Thus vaccination, T.B., Malaria & Leprosy eradication programs and the famous family planning programs are run concurrently through all primary health centres and sub-centres attached to them. Pharmacovigilance program stress the need to monitor these public health programs as many of them are overlapping and can cause ADR, drug interaction etc., on the unsuspecting, illiterate and innocent rural masses. This vigilance has to be doubled during national calamities, epidemic attacks and large gatherings of people during festivals.

   Thus, the scope of pharmacovigilance covers a range of products and people, from allopathic medicines to food and drinks and individual patient to healthcare providers, drug regulators and the government.

Advantages of Pharmacovigilance

1. It is a cost-effective method of detecting and minimising problems for patients and thereby preventing a potential disaster.
2. It functions like a safeguard against the undetected use of ineffective, substandard or counterfeit medicines and hence reduces the wastage of resources.

3. It communicates the information on the effectiveness and risks of drugs and thereby educates the health care team and the public.
4. Compared to the cost of ADR causing to a country, the cost of a pharmacovigilance program is significantly less.
5. Overall, the pharmacovigilance program ensures the safe, rational and effective use of medicines by patients.

Pharmacovigilance Practice

Pharmacovigilance program is implemented by various methods of collecting information about ADR and other drug-related problems. They are

1. Case-Control study
2. Cohort study
3. Spontaneous case report and
4. Vital statistics and record linkage study.

1. **Case-Control Study:** In this study, groups of persons with disease (cases) and groups of persons without disease (control) are compared. Here the disease selected should be due to the drug. Patient's medication histories are collected and compared, if the drug has caused the disease, its use among the cases should be many times more than the controls.

   This type of study can be conducted quickly and effectively, and that too at less cost. But it requires more scientific knowledge to conduct correctly and to interpret the data obtained after the study.

   For example, in a study of the relationship between lung cancer and cigarette smoking, it was found that the disease is 10 to 11 times more in smokers than non-smokers. As the connection between the two depends on the amount of smoking and there is very less scope for chance factor, hence the conclusion drawn from the above study is justified.

2. **Cohort Study:** A cohort is a group of people having approximately the same age and put under the same and similar conditions like receiving the same drug. In this study, the drug under study is given to the group and watched for varying periods to find out the ADR. This can be for a short period, say the treatment period plus 1 month. The study is carried out in various places in the country, and up to 2000 to 3000 patients are selected.

   Usually, toxic effects due to excessive pharmacological effects are detected by this method. Delayed effects of the drug can also be detected.

In the long-term study lasting for a few years, more patients, up to 20,000, maybe followed for detecting adverse drug reactions. Information is collected from the Doctor, Pharmacist and the patient if possible. The problem with this method is dropouts due to migration etc. It is an expensive and difficult method and known as Post Marketing Surveillance.

3. **Spontaneous Case Reports:** If a prescriber suspects some problem with the patient because of drug usage, he reports it to medical or pharmaceutical journals or to the manufacturer of the drug. This is called a spontaneous case report. Other prescribers are alerted by this method.

   Nowadays, ADR reporting agencies are available like the one with World Health Organization (WHO). Once a report is sent to them with relevant particulars, they investigate and or report it to all medical practitioners through journals, newsletters and associations etc. It is a cheaper method; however, the frequency of a particular ADR, its correlation with drugs and disease, etc., must be determined. Also, it cannot be claimed to be a complete report.

4. **Vital Statistics and Record Linkage Studies:** All the health care institutions (hospitals and clinics) and local bodies are required to maintain morbidity and mortality data. From these records, diseases prevailing and causes of death in a particular area can be collected and analysed.

   However, this method is not successful because of the long delay in collecting data, the reliability of the data etc. If the data are faithfully entered in records and computerised, it may be useful to collect and analyse them easily in future.

However, among the above 'the spontaneous case report method has been given more attention recently as it is fast and the information is given directly by the people involved. In this method, the information is either directly obtained from the patient who experiences the benefit or harm of a medicine taken or through their health care providers. The health care team also monitor for ADR while treating the patient and report if it occurs to the national pharmacovigilance centre. In some countries, the national reporting system provides for direct patient reporting. In many states of India, this is being implemented by offering a toll-free telephone number, and patients are encouraged to report any drug-related problem through this number. This type of facility will be useful when disease-specific programs are implemented. The information gathered by any of the above methods are processed by national pharmacovigilance centres and then sent to the WHO centre for International Drug Monitoring.

Conclusion

Medicines are like double-edged weapons, and to use it wisely without being hurt, vigilance is needed. If it is assured in the form National Pharmacovigilance program, it

- Increases the confidence and faith of people on medicines and health care providers.
- Provide essential information to Drug regulatory authorities so as to function more effectively and
- Educate the health care professionals about the medicine they prescribe, dispense and administer.

Thus, the pharmacovigilance program takes the entire healthcare sector one step forward towards excellence in their practice.

Questions

Short Answer Questions

1. Write a short note on the need for Pharmacovigilance.
2. List the advantages of the Pharmacovigilance program.

Long Answer Questions

3. Define Pharmacovigilance. What are its aims and scope?
4. How Pharmacovigilance program is implemented?
5. Explain the scope of Pharmacovigilance.

CHAPTER 17

MEDICATION ERRORS

Introduction

Despite care and vigilance by medical and para-medical staff, medication errors do occur. Though there are many reasons for these errors, as described below, the health care team, from treating physicians to the pharmacist to nurses, is very much concerned with such developments. In order to minimise these errors, hospitals have framed policies, rules and regulations, and strict adherence to these rules will definitely help to manage the problem.

***Definition*:** "The administration of wrong medicine or dose of medicine, diagnostic agent or chemical or treatment requiring the use of such agents to the wrong patient or at the wrong time in the wrong manner is known as a medication error."

***Classification of medication error*:** Medication error can occur at any point in time in the treatment chain, starting from prescription writing by the doctor to dispensing by a pharmacist or administration of drugs by nurses or patient's caretakers. Medication errors are very common in out-patients than in-patients for the obvious reason that out-patients compliance to instructions by the health care team is not supervised by them, and it is completely left to the patient or his caretaker who may be illiterate or negligent. However, as out-patients are usually treated for few days, due to the very nature of their disease or condition, we need to pay more attention to the patients requiring long time treatment, mainly in-patients and a few groups of out-patients with diseases requiring long time treatment like T.B, Asthma, Diabetes, Leprosy, Hypertension etc. Thus, medication errors can be classified as follows:

I. Errors in Drug Administration

A. ***Wrong dosage form*:** In this type of error, for instance, a tablet might have been given instead of an injection and vice versa. Depending upon the patient's condition, oral dosage may produce nausea, vomiting or stomach irritation, apart from delaying the onset of action by the drug. On the other hand, needless injection raises the cost of treatment.

B. ***Unordered drug is given*:** Drug not repeated in the prescription is not noted, and the previous day prescription is routinely followed, and thereby unordered drug may be administered to the patient. Not only does the patient loses the benefit of the drug written in the prescription, but also their agony is prolonged. Similar to starting of drugs at right time, stopping of them at the appropriate time is also important. Without noticing such a decision, administering the previous day's drug may complicate the treatment.

C. ***Wrong time*:** If any drug is given half an hour before or after the time specified, it is considered as the administration of the drug at the wrong time. Commonly it happens because of a basic lethargic attitude towards punctuality and interference by factors in the ward atmosphere. It may seem to be a simple error, but in some critical cases, it may lead to drug-drug interaction if the required dosing interval is not followed between drugs.

D. ***Wrong administration*:** If a drug is given through a different route than the one mentioned in the prescription, it is known as the wrong administration of the drug. One has to be careful while reading the label. Some injections have to be given only through I.M, not by I.V. Many healthcare professionals think all injections can be administered via IM or IV, depending on the emergency. It is a wrong conception as the excipients of injections differ depending on many factors, hence the wrong route may cause local irritation, swelling and dispersal problems at the site of injection.

II. Errors in Dose of Drugs

A. ***Omission of any dose*:** If a drug is not administered by the time the next dose is due, it is called the omission of dose. Nurses may fail to administer a drug, forgetfully or due to other emergencies in the ward, till the time of the next dose. If not for all drugs, for a few drugs like Digoxin and antibiotics, this may lead to complications.

B. ***Wrong Dosage*:** Correct quantity of the dose written in the prescription should be administered to the patient. Any dose above or below 5% of the correct dose is considered as the wrong dose, hence a careful measuring, counting and double reading of the prescription is a must to avoid complaints of wrong dose.

C. ***Extra dose:*** Sometimes, a patient may be given an extra dose of the prescribed medicine without checking whether the drug has been already given or not. This usually happens when it is not recorded in the medication charts immediately or during a change in duty staff at the end of working hours [shift].

Reasons for Medication Error

1. ***Engaging non-professionals*:** Medication error occurs when the members of the health care team are not able to find out while the error is being committed. Usually, it happens when non-professionals are involved in professional work where professional judgment is required. For example, if a non-pharmacist dispenses drugs, he is not able to find out incompatible drugs prescribed or how to instruct the patient about the use of those drugs without interaction. For example, when enteric-coated tablets are prescribed with alkaline drugs, they have to be taken with a minimum of half an hour gap, otherwise, the enteric coating breaks in the stomach itself instead of the intestine and releases the drug in the stomach, which may irritate the stomach or become useless for the patient. Thus, anyone who can read the prescription cannot dispense the prescription as claimed by a few vested interests in the field.
2. ***Inadequate labelling*:** Insufficient information on the label leads to medication errors. All the necessary information, like dose, route of administration, expiry date, storage etc., should be mentioned on the label, otherwise, patients tend to assume things and consume the drugs as they presume. Important points like 'Poison', 'caution' or 'warning' have to be highlighted in labels. They are printed in a red or different colour to attract the attention of the patients, or auxiliary labels have to be affixed on the containers. This information is very much important and useful even to nurses in the ward who are in a hurry or hard-pressed for time. Sometimes, 'pictograms' [pictures] are fixed on the containers to help the illiterate patients.
3. ***Non-reporting of medication error*:** Majority of the people try to hide their mistakes; the healthcare team is not an exemption. Thus, any medication error or untoward incidence is not reported to the hospital administration to take remedial measures immediately. Many people think it is an unnecessary headache to report such errors, even if it occurs due to some other reason than their fault. Thus prevention, treatment, correction and subsequent benefits are denied to the patient, and for that, inadequate hospital policies have to be blamed. Correct policies encourage people to be truthful so as to report incidents inwards. An incident is any happening which is not consistent with the routine operation of the hospital or the routine care of the patient. It may be an accident or situation which might result in an accident. If an incident is not reported, it goes uninvestigated, and thereby the chance for detecting its real reason is diminished. Thus, without knowing the root cause, the

team loses foresight if it occurs at another time for the same patient or other patient. Hence this time and every time, they fail in preventing similar medical errors. Thus, the absence of proper education and policies by hospital administration, inculcated in the health care team, is one of the reasons for medical error.

Minimising Medication Error

Medication error can be prevented to a maximum extent, but it is difficult to eliminate altogether. Though the aim is to have zero error in all treatments, errors do creep in due to human factors. But its frequency can be reduced. The reasons for medication errors are listed above, if the shortfalls pointed out in those reasons are corrected, medication errors can be avoided to a larger extent. Thus, engaging only pharmacists for handling drugs, good dispensing practices by way of adequate labelling and faithful reporting of errors etc., help the hospital administration to minimise medication errors.

Apart from the above, pharmacists and nurses can help avoid medication error by co-o works. Pharmacists – if appointed inwards – can prepare patient medication profile cards for each in-patient in which he can record a list of drugs given, allergy, possible drug-drug interactions, precautions to be followed etc., which can be viewed by nurses before administering drugs. Similarly, nurses, while preparing to administer drugs to the patient, should

1. verify whether the medicine was already given
2. collect the drug from the cub board, read the label 2 or 3 times, and check the content for physical stability
3. discard any balance leftover medicines and
4. check whether the previous medicine or dose is incompatible with the present one.

During the administration of medicine, nurses should once again verify all the information. The medicine should be prepared just a few minutes before administration. Patient should be properly identified, and she should wait until the administration of medicine is completed [except LVP]. Then she should write 'given' on the medication card against the name and time of the drug and put her initials.

If the above regulations are followed sincerely, medication errors can be reduced to a very minimum, and the patient who is already suffering from his disease can be saved from unnecessary trouble and problems. Apart from the above few other methods are followed nowadays to minimise the medication errors that are described below.

Lasa Drugs and Tall Man Lettering

LASA drugs are those drugs which *look alike* in physical appearance and *sound alike* drugs are similar when pronounced. Looks alike drugs may have even similar packing or colour, and sound-alike drugs are with similar spellings except for a few letters.

Worldwide thousands of new drugs are marketed every week. In India, too, hundreds of formulations are introduced within a short period, and hence there is a huge possibility for the introduction of LASA drugs. Hence World Health Organization's international non-proprietary names expert group works to develop international non-proprietary names for pharmaceutical substances for acceptance worldwide. Similarly, various countries, including India, took efforts to prevent the marketing of LASA drugs.

LASA drugs invariably lead to medication errors by dispensing the wrong drug. This error may be due to any one of the following reasons.

1. Similar packing or labelling
2. Illegible handwriting in prescriptions
3. New products introduction and subsequent incomplete knowledge of drug names by doctors and pharmacists and
4. Confusing factors like similar clinical use, similar strength and dosage forms.

Medication errors due to LASA drugs can be avoided by following some important procedures or strategies by the pharmacists. They are,

1. Avoiding purchase and stocking of those drugs
2. If a new formulation or dosage form is introduced, it should be compared with existing drugs to find out similarities, if any.
3. Additional warning labels can be fixed over the LASA drugs.
4. Prescription should be legibly written or typed or written in capital letters as per the latest Govt. of India instructions
5. While dispensing pharmacist must read the label of the drug thrice while taking it from the cub board while dispensing and while packing before giving it to the patient.
6. LASA pair drugs should be stored far away from each other
7. LASA drugs list should be prepared, updated periodically and circulated among the pharmacists. The list can also be displayed on the pharmacy staff notice board.
8. Educate the patients about the drugs they are taking. If they notice any difference in it, they will enquire. It is better if they are able to tell their drug's name

9. All previous errors encountered in LASA drugs by the healthcare team should be tabulated and evaluated periodically.
10. In this computer age, it is possible to prevent the entry or licensing of LASA drugs by the approving or licensing authorities.

Examples for LASA drugs are

Lovastatin	--	Loratadine
Chlorpromazine	--	Carbamazepine
Cotrimoxazole	--	Clotrimazole
Carbimazole	--	Cotrimoxazole
Difflam	--	Daflon
Cycloserine	--	Cyclosporine

This is about sound alike drugs, look alike on the other hand, depends on the pharmaceutical manufacturer's design, printed label, and size and shape of the drug which differs from region to region and country to country. Hence, they should be physically compared and noted.

Tall Man Lettering

Institute for Safe Medication practice [ISMP] has developed a method to prevent the medication errors because of similar, sound-alike drugs. As already pointed out above, a similar sound is due to almost similar spelling. ISMP method is for differentiating the unique letter characters of similar drug names known to have confused with one another. "Starting with a name printed in lowercase letters, tall man lettering highlights the differences between similar drug names by capitalizing dissimilar letters. Accentuating a unique portion of a drug name with uppercase letters along with other means such as colour, bolding, or contrast can draw attention to the dissimilarities between look-alike [sound alike] drug names as well as alert health care providers that the drug name can be confused with another drug name" according to ISMP.

This method has reduced medication errors, it was found by many studies and surveys. Hence this method is supported by the Food and Drug Administration of the USA and other organizations like WHO and the International Medication Safety Network [IMSN]. In the above survey, participants referred to the tall man letters as a "Visual Alert System" and "Subconscious cue" that helps to refocus the eye and "slow down or stop" the process to ensure they have the correct drug.

ISMP updates its list of drugs name pairs periodically with recommended bolded tall man letters. This list is prepared by analysing the error database of ISMP, surveys with doctors and internal assessments. In a follow-up study by ISMP majority of people [about 86%] who participated in it felt the use of tall man lettering helped reduce the risk of errors among medications with look-alike names.

Some examples of Tall man [Capital Letters] pairs are

HydrALAZINE	--	hydrOXYzine
OxyCONTIN	--	oxyCODONE/ HYDROcodone
MetyroSINE	--	metyraPONE
RaNITIdine	--	riMANTAdine
CarBAMAzepine	--	carBIMAzole
CefOTAXime	--	cefTAZIDime
ChlorproMAZINE	--	chlorproPAMIDE
LOsartan	--	LOVAstatin
NeuroBION	--	neuroNTIN
NiFEDIpine	--	niMODIpine

Questions

Short Answer Questions

1. Classify medication errors
2. What are LASA drugs?
3. What is the meaning for Tall man drugs?

Long Answer Questions

4. Define medication error. What are the reasons for it? How it can be minimised?
5. Explain LASA dugs with examples
6. Explain Tall man drugs with examples

CHAPTER 18

DRUG INTERACTIONS

Introduction

Though drug interactions are part of adverse drug reactions, it is studied separately because of its importance. Concurrent administration of many drugs to the patient is a reality, and hence the possibility of drug interactions is always there. Invariably almost all the drugs are synthetic chemicals or chemical constituents of natural drugs, and hence the potential for drug interactions is evident. Moreover, these chemicals are administered into the body, where scores of biochemicals are already present, and also, the chemical drugs given from outside is metabolised to different chemicals inside the body. Thus, we mix up a lot of chemicals in the patient's body, and if we ignore this or are non-vigilant throughout the course of long treatment, harmful effects cannot be avoided.

Definition: Drug interaction is defined as a situation in which the effects of one drug are altered by prior or co-administration of another drug. It also includes drug-food interactions and drug-disease interactions.

Reasons for Drug Interactions

1. ***Patients go to many physicians:*** Patients are in a hurry to get relief from their disease, and hence they go to many physicians and even to many systems of treatment like Ayurveda, Siddha or Homeopathy. Because of this situation, there are chances for adverse drug interactions, but usually, patients purchase drugs from neighbourhood pharmacies only, and hence pharmacists can counsel such patients.
2. ***Simultaneous use of OTC drugs and prescription drugs:*** Patients purchase some drugs for their common problems from nearby pharmacies, and they continue to use the same along with prescription drugs. They may not reveal it to the physician or pharmacist; hence, questions are asked cleverly using symptoms normally treated with OTC drugs and information collected.

3. ***Non-compliance:*** Instructions given by doctors or pharmacists regarding the use of drugs are not correctly followed by many patients, which needs attention to avoid drug-drug interactions.
4. ***Drug potency:*** If potent drugs are used together, the chances of harmful effects are more. For example, if antipsychotic, antidepressant and anti-parkinsonism agents with anticholinergic activity are used together, dryness of mouth and blurring of vision result.
5. ***Drug abuse:*** Few patients are abusing drugs knowingly or unknowingly, and hence interactions chances increase.

Problems in Detecting Drug Interactions

Patient's disease conditions are too complicated to detect ADR. If something abnormal is detected, it is considered a disease manifestation and not a probable ADR. Sometimes, they are attributed to factors other than drug interaction, like tolerance, irregular use of drug etc.

The index of suspicion of many clinicians is low, as they believe nothing will be wrong with their treatment. Only when the problem becomes big do they search for earlier reports of ADR of drugs used, until then, they doubt their own observation of symptoms of ADR.

For many drugs, there is no measure for an activity similar to antihypertension and hypoglycemic drugs, which are measured by blood pressure and blood sugar level, respectively. For example, take the case of tranquillisers and analgesics, whose effect potential is impossible to detect.

Above all, if drug interaction in a patient is reported by a physician, he will be in a critical situation where criticism and possible legal actions may result. Hence nobody wants to be in such a bad situation because of their own reporting.

Uses of Drug Interaction Reports

If the interaction between two drugs is known, therapeutic alternatives can be used. For example, the anticoagulant drug Warfarin interacts with Aspirin, hence it can be given with paracetamol instead of aspirin. Similarly, if tetracycline and antacids have to be given together, it can be done with a time gap. Thus, interacting drugs are given by following adjustments like changing doses or close monitoring of therapy etc.

Some interactions are beneficial so that these interactions can be used to the advantage of patients. For instance, probenecid, if given together with penicillin, the duration of action of the latter is increased. Hence the dose of penicillin is reduced.

All reported drug interactions need not produce the same effect in all patients. It varies depending on many variables like age, genetics, renal disease, hepatic disorders, drinking habit, smoking, food intake etc. Each of these variables influences the effect of the drug, therefore, drugs interactions reports should be used depending on the present case. Moreover, some interactions are reported based on animal studies; they need not be the same in the human body.

It was found that if a person is exposed to DDT pesticides, the metabolism of some drugs is affected. Thus, even if the environment can affect the drug's activity, hence need for dose or therapy adjustment is clear.

Types of Drug Interactions

Depending on the benefit or otherwise of a drug interaction, they are classified into two types:

1. Beneficial interactions and
2. Adverse interactions

1. ***Beneficial interactions***: Few drugs, on interaction with other drugs, produce beneficial effects. Potentiation or synergisms are some of the examples of such benefits. Some drugs are used deliberately to enhance the effect of other drugs or minimise the unwanted effect of it. The examples are the sulphamethoxazole and trimethoprim combination and carbidopa and levodopa, respectively. There are many formulations in the market using these beneficial effects, like estrogen–progestogen combination as a contraceptive, ampicillin, cloxacillin combination as potent antibiotic and β.blockers – a diuretic combination as hypotensive agents.

   Drug interactions can also be used to treat drug over- dose patients, as they nullify or antagonise the adverse effect of overdose drugs. Examples are levodopa and vitamin B_6, warfarin and vitamin K, narcotic analgesics and nalorphine.

2. ***Adverse interactions:*** As newer and newer chemicals are introduced for doctors to treat patients, and multiple drugs are commonly prescribed, the possibility for adverse interactions also increases day by day. These adverse reactions can be put under two broad classifications, namely,

   1. Pharmacodynamic drug interactions and
   2. Pharmacokinetic drug interactions

   If drug interactions are based on their effect on the body, they are called pharmacodynamic drug interactions, and if they are due to the absorption, distribution, metabolism or excretion of the drug, they are referred to as pharmacokinetic interactions.

1. **Pharmacodynamic Drug Interactions**

   These interactions happen when two drugs with the same effects are concurrently administered unknowingly. All the beneficial interactions listed above are also based on the activity of drugs only. Some adverse interactions due to drug activities are listed below.

   If hypnotics are given with antihistamines or narcotic analgesics or tranquillizers, or alcohol, their effect is increased drastically, resulting in unwanted proportions. Hence combinations of CNS depressants should be avoided, but sometimes it, is overlooked or hidden from prescribers.

   Digoxin and quinidine combination is another example for pharmacy dynamic drug interaction. Basic properties of all the drugs prescribed should be remembered by prescribers and pharmacists to avoid such problems.

2. **Pharmacokinetic Drug Interactions**

   These interactions are due to

   1. Change in the absorption of drugs
   2. Alteration in protein binding and distribution
   3. Biotransformation changes and
   4. Drug elimination problems

      (i) ***Change in the absorption of drugs*:** Iron preparations and drugs containing calcium, magnesium and aluminium (antacids) precipitate or chelate tetracyclines, hence its absorption from the GI tract is affected. Propanthelene, if administered along with digoxin or pethidine its absorption is delayed or reduced.

      (ii) ***Alteration in distribution*:** If chloral hydrate is given with warfarin, trichloro acetic acid, the metabolite of the former displaces the warfarin from its protein binding sites. Hence Warfarin concentration in the blood increases to double the quantity. However, it is temporary as clearance increases correspondingly.

      (iii) ***Biotransformation changes*:** Some drugs increase the drug-metabolizing enzymes, and some others decrease it. Hence there are changes in plasma drug concentration and drug's activity which either decreases or increases. If the given drug produces pharmacological activity, it is reduced by the induction of enzymes, and if the metabolite is responsible for the drug's activity, it is increased. Example is the co-administration of phenylbutazone and phenytoin. Here phenytoin effect is increased by the induction of enzyme by phenylbutazone. Like this, when allopurinol and 6. mercaptopurine are given together, metabolising enzymes are inhibited by Allopurinol, hence, 6 mercaptopurine metabolism is delayed, and its toxic effect increases. Dose of 6. mercaptopurine should be reduced in such cases.

(iv) ***Drug elimination problems***: Some drugs, if administered together, compete for elimination via active tubular secretion. As a result, each of these drugs eliminates slowly and consequently stays longer inside the body. Duration of action thus increases. One example already given is probenecid and penicillin, and another one is salicylates and uricosuric agents.

If we alter the pH of the urine, the drug's elimination is affected. This type of drug interaction is used for treating poison cases. For example, if we make urine pH alkaline using sodium bicarbonate, acidic drugs like salicylates and phenobarbitone are eliminated quickly from the body. Similarly, if we make urine pH acidic using ammonium chloride, alkaline drugs like quinidine are eliminated faster.

CLASSIFICATION OF DRUG INTERACTIONS

- Beneficial interactions
  - To minimize risk
  - To improve efficiency (potentiation and synergism)
- Adverse interactions
  - Pharmacodynamic drug interactions
  - Pharmacokinetic drug interactions
    1. Change in absorption
    2. Alteration in distribution
    3. Biotransformation changes
    4. Elimination problems

Drug Interaction Examples

I. Analgesics	
1. Aspirin with Alcohol	GI irritation and bleeding
2. Aspirin with Ibuprofen	No superior action
3. Narcotic analgesics with CNS depressants like barbiturates	Excessive depressant action
4. Paracetamol with Metoclopramide	Increased onset of Paracetamol action
II. Cardio Vascular Agents	
1. Digitalis and its preparations with barbiturates	Increase the metabolism of Digoxin hence, more dose may be required

Table *Contd...*

2. Digitalis and its preparations with Diuretics	Potassium depletion, give KCl tablets. If not, heart become sensitive to Digitalis and its toxicity
3. Digitalis and its preparations with Reserpine	Increased risk of cardiac arrest
4. Methyl Dopa with Levodopa	Potentiation, so reduce dose.
5. Propranolol with Insulin, Tolbutamide etc.	Increase the action of hypoglycemic agents, results in acute hypoglycemia. Additional danger is that effect is not noticeable till serious stage
6. Anticoagulants Warfarin etc. with	
(a) Aspirin	Increased effect
(b) Antacids	Decreased effect
(c) Chloramphenicol	Increased effect
(d) Phenylbutazone and oxyphenbutazone	Increase anticoagulant effect
(e) Phenytoin	Phenytoin effect increases, anticoagulant effect decreases
(f) Vitamin K	Antagonism
III. GI Agents	
1. Antacids with Bisacodyl	GI irritation due to disintegration of enteric coating in stomach itself.
2. Antacids with Tetracycline	Metal ions in antacids like Ca, Mg, Al form complex with Tetracycline, so poor absorption
IV. Hypoglycemic Agents	
Insulin, Tolbutamide, etc. with 1. Corticosteroids like Prednisolone	Increase the blood glucose level
2. Alcohol	Different effects with various intake quantities, may induce faster hypoglycemia
3. Propranolol	Increase the action of insulin etc.
4. Coumarin (anticoagulant)	Increase in action due to decrease in metabolism. Reduce dose.
5. Phenylbutazone	Increase the action, so reduce dose
V. Psychopharmacological Agents	
With alcohol	More CNS Depressant action. Hence avoid it.
1. Antidepressants with	
(a) Coumarin	Increase the effect of anti-coagulants
(b) MAO inhibitors	Tremors, convulsions
(c) Reserpine	Contraindicated
2. Antipsychotic agents (chlorpromazine group) with	
(a) Antacids	Magnesium trisilicate decrease plasma level of the drug. Avoid or delay
(b) Anticholinergics	Dryness of mouth, blurring of vision, constipation, and urine detention
(c) Levodopa	Action of Levodopa inhibited
(d) MAO Inhibitors	Increase the action of the antipsychotic drugs

3. Sedatives and Hypnotics with	
(a) Alcohol	Enhanced CNS depression
(b) MAO inhibitors	Enhanced CNS depression so avoid it
(c) Digitoxin	Increase the rate of metabolism of Digitoxin
(d) Griseofulvin	Decrease in action of Griseofulvin
VI. Vitamins	
1. Folic acid with Phenytoin	Development of Folic acid deficiency and reduced Phenytoin level
2. Vitamin B_6 with Levodopa	Antagonism patients under Levodopa therapy should avoid multivitamins
3. Vitamin C with Aspirin	Reduced Vitamin C absorption
4. Vitamin D with Phenytoin	Increase the metabolism of Vitamin D, so Vitamin D deficiency (Rickets, etc.)
5. Vitamin K with Coumarin	Antagonism

Questions

Short Answer Questions

1. Define Drug-Drug interaction and what are the two types of Drug Interactions?
2. What are the reasons for Drug-Drug Interactions?
3. What are the problems in detecting drug interactions?
4. How can we use the Drug Interaction information?

Long Answer Questions

5. Classify drug interactions. Explain each one of them with examples.
6. What are pharmacokinetic drug interactions? Give examples.

REFERENCE BOOKS AND WEBSITES

1. Remington's 'Pharmaceutical sciences' – 18th Edition
2. 'Hospital Pharmacy' by William E.Hassan 4th Edition
3. 'Clinical Pharmacy and Hospital Drugs Management' by David H.Lawson and Michael E.Richard.
4. Oxford's 'Text book of Clinical Pharmacology and Drug therapy' by D.S Graham Smith and J.K. Armson
5. British National Formulary
6. 'The Pharmacological basis of Therapeutics' by Louis S.Goodmann and Alfred Gilmann
7. 'Avery's Drug treatment' 3rd Edition Edited by Trevor M.Speight
8. 'Text book of Therapeutics' by Herfindal and Gourley, 6th Edition
9. 'Pharmaceutical Practice' by Richard and Winfeild
10. 'Medical Pharmacology' by K.D Thirupathi
11. 'A Text Book of Clinical Pharmacy Practice, Edited by G.Parthasarathi,
12. Remington: The science and Practice of Pharmacy' 19th & 22nd Editions
13. 'Pharmacist's Drug Hand Book'- American Society of Health System Pharmacists
14. 'Clinical Pharmacy and Therapeutics' 4th Edition – Eric T.Herfindal, et al
15. www.who.int
16. www.ncbi.nlm.nih.gov
17. www.nun.ca
18. www.fda.gov
19. www.ajhp.org
20. www.en.wikipedia.org
21. www.student.bmj.com
22. www.lifetechnologies.com
23. www.medilexicon.com
24. http://quizlet.com
25. http://nih.gov

www.ingramcontent.com/pod-product-compliance
Lightning Source LLC
Chambersburg PA
CBHW071331230926
51849CB00002B/370
* 9 7 8 9 3 9 0 2 1 1 9 1 3 *